Journey into Your Soul

finding your true self

Journey into Your Soul

finding your true self

Liane Rich

The information contained in this book is not intended as a substitute for professional advice. Neither the publisher nor the author is engaged in rendering professional advice to the reader. The intent of the author is only to offer information of a general nature to assist you in your quest for emotional and spiritual well-being. In the event you use any of the information in this book for yourself, the author and the publisher assume no responsibility for your actions.

Loving Light Books
Copyright © 2024 Liane Rich

ISBN 13: 978-1-878480-35-4
ISBN 10: 1-878480-35-9

Loving Light Books
www.lovinglightbooks.com
Also Available at:
Amazon: www.amazon.com

for my soul friend, Frances

Author's Note

What would you do if you heard a very loud voice telling you that it was God and that it wanted your help to write a book? That's pretty much how it started for me about 35 years ago.

For those of you who are new to God's books and curious to know more about the source of this information, I have published a small book titled, *For the Love of God: An Introduction to God.* This small book will give you a great deal of insight into this voice that speaks to me and writes through me.

For the Love of God: An Introduction to God also appears as the Introduction to our book titled, *The Book of Love.* Either book will give you greater insight into this voice and the source of this information.

In the back of this book you will find a brief description of my first encounter with the God voice as well as a full list of book titles. I am told that repetition is used as a teaching tool in these books. God uses repetition freely and says that's the fastest way to get through our judgmental, conscious mind to the subconscious.

I hand write (channel) each book and type them myself. There is no editing of this material, so you are reading the original version as it was channeled by me. I think of this information as God giving me my own personal answers and guiding me to a more fulfilling life. I hope you enjoy the insights presented here and that they may help you in some small way to have a happier, healthier and more peaceful life.

In Loving Light, *Liane*

Preface

Once you begin to heal, you will begin to feel more love. Love is the answer to absolutely everything.

I am God and I am asking you to heal. Why would God ask you to heal? Simply because you are from me and you are part of me. So – what is healing and how does healing take place? The first thing to remember is that you are human and you are spirit. You heal physically and you heal spiritually. You also heal emotionally and mentally. Now is a time that has been called the grand awakening. It is a time of learning and growing. It is also a time of knowing or becoming who you truly are. You are part of God and it is a good idea to begin to admit this to yourself.

So, what does it mean to be God? It simply means that you are a spiritual being that has come forth from a spiritual being of loving light. You are a form of energy that is moving and changing and growing. You move and you change and you grow simply because you *are* energy. You are an energy force that inhabits a human form or body. You do not exist as simply a body or simply a spirit. You are both.

You are light and you are form. You are energy and thoughts and emotions and you move and expel thoughts and emotions. In the expelling of thoughts and emotions, you actually "create" more of what you are. You send out signals and you send out thoughts and you form words and express your ideas. You are a "creative being," and you literally create a personal environment made up of all the energy, including thoughts, ideas and emotions that you are sending out. You create the personal world that you exist within by simply expelling, or expressing, your personal beliefs and ideas and emotions. You are a creating, expressing machine. You do it all and then you ask "Why – why is this happening?"

In this book I will try to explain for you "why this is happening." I will give you as much insight into this whole situation as is possible at this time. It is not often that you hear from God and it is with gratitude that I communicate to you.

Sit back, relax and enjoy this journey into your soul... the part of you who will save you from your own creations.

Liane: Thank you God. Do you have a title?

God: Yes – *Journey into Your Soul* is good. Subtitle is *finding your true self.* Yes – this is good!

I wish to explain this technique of writing: I choose to channel energy through Liane in such a way that will affect her energy and thoughts and ideas about life. This energy is actually a signal, or vibration, that travels from her brain down her arm and forms words on a page. She does not understand how this works and has never asked.

The information that I have given in this book, and in all others, is written in a manner that will affect your emotional and mental bodies. This information is given in the simplest form in an effort to bypass your more complex mind. You love complexity and you are constantly wanting more. I give you simplicity which bypasses your conscious self and makes its way into your subconscious.

Liane often struggles with wanting to correct sentence structure and certain words, but I have convinced her to allow my way of communicating with you to stay. You will find this simplistic style of writing very direct, to the point and sometimes even childlike. It is my way of getting through to your subconscious and it works well for where you now are in your evolution. I hope you enjoy this information and that you may learn to love and accept your wonderful soul self.

God

"All God's books are designed to draw you within to your own God self."

Introduction

When you begin your rise in awareness, you will automatically begin to feel changes in your mental and your emotional bodies. These changes will eventually manifest through your physical body. At some point you will begin to feel like a different person. You will still be "you," however you will have added to you. You will expand your scope of understanding and you will gain insight that was previously unavailable to you. This is you waking up! This is you beginning to rise up! This is being done on a grand scale and it is a most sought after experience. Souls come to earth to experience many things and this is just one of those many things.

So, as you begin this process of awakening, you will change. Herein lies the problem for many of you. You do not like change and you do not like flowing with energy. You like to block energy and you love to control energy. This may cause discomfort for many of you. What you are doing in this grand awakening is shifting from your human side to your spirit side. You are shifting your perspective from that of human fear to that of spirit love. You are literally moving into a part of you that is unconditional acceptance and love. This part has always been with you, or in you, you are just now becoming aware of it and the fact that you are a soul as well as a body.

So now we have you beginning to wake up to the fact that you are more than just human, and you may get a little confused as to who you truly are. You are so vast that you may not explore, or discover, all that you are in just one lifetime. So you return many times to this third dimension in an effort to wake up, or become aware of the many parts of you. It is not necessary to wake up to all of these many parts, however you are an inquisitive being and you love creating and discovering new things. Many times you create new things or situations just to see how they make you feel.

You see, you are a feeling being and this fact leads you to express and explore your emotions. You have literally created an emotional body where you store all these dynamic feelings. One of the most essential parts of healing is to heal the emotions. We heal our emotions by feeling them and allowing them to be useful and an asset. If you begin to deny your emotions, you literally shut them down. You may close down an emotion to the point that it no longer serves you. All emotions serve a purpose and are simply sending you a signal as to what is bothering you, or what is pleasing you. You then determine how to respond to any received emotion. If you act out an emotion it could cause complications for you. If you release your emotions in a productive way it could assist you.

So emotions are simply a signal that you have some built up emotional energy in your emotional body. The problem comes when you are overwhelmed emotionally and you become frightened of the energy being emitted by emotions. This could be fear energy or it could be anger. It could even be love. Many of you are afraid of love and this may cause complications for you. One of the biggest complications is the fact that you (your true self) are love. You are literally love energy that is all accepting and unconditional in nature. Can you imagine a human who is really an energy being who is "all accepting and unconditional love?" What problem might such a being have when navigating the material world where all these humans (with hidden emotional bodies) live and play and create?

This is the subject of this book titled *Journey into Your Soul: finding your true self.* I hope you enjoy it.

God

$\mathcal{A}$s you begin to rise in awareness, you will begin to change your vibration. Your vibration is your rate or speed of fluctuation and movement. You literally fluctuate back and forth from your Source (God) to your body. You are constantly and continually moving. You are literally a vibrating, creating machine. You feel like you are physical and emotional and mental but you are so much more.

As you raise your vibration, you are able to spend more time in your Source. You are able to calm your fears and you are able to be at peace. Peace allows you to see situations in your life, and in the lives of others, in a whole new way. Peace allows for calmness to set in and calmness allows you to un-tense and begin to relax. How relaxed would you say that you are? Are you calm and at peace? Can you see your life from a perspective of peace? Peace knows love, and love is unconditional acceptance. Once you find this state of love, you will feel quite pleasant and quite pleased with your life. You will begin to appreciate all that you have and all that you are. You will no longer find fault and you will know that all is well.

This is your soul's goal. Your soul wishes to come through the fear and mistrust and anger and concern for your safety. Your soul wants to rise above to a state of joy and love. Your soul is God. God is love and God is eternal and God is all knowing. This allows God to be aware that all is well and there are no problems. There are no problems simply because everything here in this third dimension is simply a thought that is manifesting. A thought manifests (or solidifies) by energy building up in it. This allows a thought to grow and expand and take on a life of its own. This allows individual creators to send out more of the same thought to expand the original thought even more. The more energy that is put into a thought, the bigger it gets. This is similar to blowing up a big balloon and is simply physics… the more energy you put into something, the bigger it gets.

So – do you have an enemy? How much energy are you putting into that enemy? How are you (that creating machine that is you) making your enemy bigger, greater, more dangerous? And if others do not put their "energy" into your enemy, do you find ways to convince them to fear what you fear? And if you cannot convince them to fear what you fear, do you then begin to mistrust and fear them? How many enemies are you creating without even realizing what you are creating? Do you know that you are an energy being come from God? Do you realize that you have the power to create by sending out thought energy? Have you bothered to study the physics of this dimension? Do you know who you are and where you came from?

You are a spirit. You are a soul who inhabits every cell and every atom of this body that you are in. You come from God! God is not a man in the sky. God is "creative" energy. God creates! You are made up of the same stuff (creative energy) that is God. How can you turn off what you are? You cannot! You may go unconscious of what and who you are but you cannot turn off you. You are a creative energy being!

Once in awhile I get your attention and we begin to exchange ideas and thoughts. In these moments you will feel uplifted and good. You love inspiration and that is due to the fact that inspiration comes from God, your Source.

As you go along in life, God/spirit/soul is constantly trying to reach out to you. You are from God and you are spirit and soul in a human body. So why can't you seem to connect with all that you are? We must take you back to the beginning in order to answer this question. "In the beginning God created heaven and earth." Oh wait – that's not really what took place. In the beginning God began to move. God took on shape by movement and because God is light energy, God began to vibrate and to explore all that God contains. And what does God contain? In essence, God contains absolutely everything that is or could possibly be.

So, God is full of everything and nothing exists but God. Where does that leave you, the soul that is you? You must be part of this energy or light that is God. Nothing exists outside of God so that makes you and everyone else part of God. You love knowing that you are part of God energy or an expression of God, but you are not so crazy with the idea that all others are from and part of God. And if all others are part of and from God that means all others are part of you. That is what I most want you to understand so you will calm down and stop hurting yourselves and others. You are part of the same energy field. Energy moves in waves and exists in waves. There are no fences or boundaries for energy. Energy moves and flows and expands and contracts. It is light moving through matter.

So, we have this energy field and it contains all that exists and it has no beginning and no end. It is everlasting, loving light and it is in you as well as outside of you. If you draw a picture of light you get the idea a little. Light shines openly until it hits an object that blocks the light. When light hits an object it creates a shadow. Shadows exist because matter is denser than light. Light cannot penetrate matter without blowing it apart. Matter is dense, or a much slower vibration than light, so light must slowly and gradually merge with matter.

This merging of light and matter takes some time. Like I said, light must oh so gradually "enter" or merge with matter or there may be big complications. You are light energy and you are human matter. You are the light who has entered a human form and is oh so gradually "merging" and entering it. You are complex light come from God (all that is) and you are entering you (human form) and taking over as you enter more fully. God is entering matter and, in doing so, big changes are occurring, and denser energies are being uprooted and beginning to lighten up or shed their denseness. The light vibrates faster than the denser, dark energy and it causes these thicker energies to begin to crumble. Once dense energy crumbles, it is easier to move. In this case, the denser energy becomes smaller and less heavy. Once the denser energy is light enough, it may begin to float to the surface where it can be observed.

All energy is rising and being made visible at this time. Why? Because you (God you) are entering matter (human you). You are God who is more fully entering God's creation. You create by sending out thoughts and ideas. Over time, your stream of light continues to flow "into" your creations. You literally move into what you create. You all do this and you are all experiencing the breakdown of dense energy as the light that is you enters you more fully.

"We are all God. Since there was nothing but God before the universe began, and since the universe was created by God, from the substance of God, how could we be anything else?"

–Unknown

---

*A*s you continue to awaken, you will continue to change. The greatest change will be emotional. You will become more sensitive to energy. This will allow you to be more sensitive to your own feelings. As you feel more strongly you will, or may, feel the need to yell at everyone who is doing anything remotely wrong. You may become more fearful and angrier. This will be due to the fact that, as you take in more light energy, you will be disturbing more dense energy. This energy that is dense may have been with you since childhood or it may go back into past lives. All lives affect you in some way. You don't have to remember the past for it to affect you.

So, as you rise in awareness, you may feel a tug-of-war within you. In one way you are feeling more loving due to light energy entering you more fully, and in another way, you are feeling the denser energies that are breaking down and coming, or rising, to the surface. This is all a process that is taking place and affecting you physically. The main thing is to stay calm and know that you are healing and rising up. It is also a good idea to remember that many others are being affected by the increase in light energy as it causes the dense energy to crumble and rise to the surface. This is a good thing; it just may not feel good or look good to you now.

As this process of taking on light continues, you will begin to see many changes in people in general. Everyone will respond in their own way depending upon their own personal fears and beliefs. Every human has experienced their own personal situations and events that have helped to form their personality and how they might view life at this particular time. No two people share identical experiences and therefore have formed identical belief systems. Belief systems are usually formed by layer upon layer of thoughts that are held on to tightly – sometimes lifetime after lifetime. Usually the thoughts that are held on to tightly, and therefore wired in place, are the more fearful thoughts. These are thoughts that warn you about danger and they are set in place in an effort to protect your vulnerabilities and help to keep you safe.

Most of your more fearful thoughts have been interwoven with less fearful childhood thoughts that turn into beliefs. Such small thoughts as "there's a monster under my bed" turn into bigger thoughts like, "there are monsters outside, I shouldn't go out there." These thoughts, once solidified, turn to bigger more fearful thoughts like, "there are monsters lying to me and they want to hurt me in some way." All fearful thoughts have the ability to grow in size and become paranoia. It just takes time. Put enough energy (thought energy) into a particular belief and then, voila`, you have created your personal creation, or reality, that you now get to live in.

Thought creates. You are a creative being and you create using thought energy. So, what do you want to think about today and solidify as part of your world? You get to choose every day what you will focus on and what energy you will add to this world. You are a creating machine who is totally unaware of what it is doing. Wake up! The time is now for you to make conscious choices as to what you wish to put your creative energy into. The more you focus your thoughts on something, the bigger it will get. Why? Because you are feeding it energy. It is just like watering a plant... water will help it grow. Water only the things that you love and want to see grow.

❧

*F*or the most part, you are the most loving energy. You carry this love energy in every cell and atom of your body. You are a loving light being that exists and inhabits a human form. Your biology is made up of billions and trillions of energy particles. You are also connected to a massive, never-ending field of light! You are the most creative and most powerful form of life in this third dimension.

So, if you are so strong, how is it that you are so weak and vulnerable? You are a process of life. You are a movement of life. You are an energy that is growing and constantly changing. You are so intricate in design, and your science has not yet discovered all of your potential. You are a mystery in the making. You are moving and growing and changing and you are made up mostly of energy. You contain very little matter and you contain mostly creative energy that is alive and moving. You are a vibrating, oscillating machine, and you have no idea that this part of you is running and working behind the scenes. You think you are one thing when you are actually many, many things. It is like owning a very complex computer but you only know how to turn it on and maybe off. You do not know all that you can, and sometimes do, create with your computer. You have no instruction manual and so you must play around until you find options that work for you.

Now; once you learn the basics of your computer, it will be easier to discover and learn the more complex parts. This is known as growth or becoming "aware." This awareness is part of waking up and this is the "grand awakening." We are in the process of this grand awakening now. We are learning how to be spirit as well as body and mind. We are learning to grow in love which is our true self, our true source. We are waking up to the fact that we may be much more than we have been told. There are many who are choosing to wake up at this time. Others of you will continue to sleep, or remain unconscious of their many talents and creative abilities. All souls enter earth with a plan or purpose, even if that purpose is just to have fun and create some mischief. If you have entered to enjoy yourself in this manner, you will probably not be interested in reading a book titled *Journey into Your Soul: finding your true self.* If, on the other hand, you are searching for greater awareness, this may assist you in your quest. All information given here is meant to assist in waking you up and allowing you, or assisting you, in making more conscious choices. After all, you live inside of you and you don't seem to know a lot about "you."

You have actually been on a self-discovery journey since you entered earth. At one point you learned that you could keep your balance enough to stand and walk. Many of you learned to keep your balance well enough to ride a bike or to roller skate. Now you wish to learn to keep your balance well enough that you might "rise up." To do this rising up technique it is important to keep your balance and not lean too far to the left or the right. Try, at all times, to stay calm and balanced in the center. This will assist you "if" your goal is to rise up at this time.

❧

$\mathcal{A}$s you continue to wake up to the fact that you are energy, you will begin to adjust your thoughts. Thoughts do have power! They have the power and the ability to move you in one direction or another. It takes a little time to learn to create and move in positive ways. Mostly it takes becoming accustomed to change. If you can learn to flow with your life you will feel better. It is a matter of letting go and enjoying the ride.

Most times you try to control all that is occurring in an effort to feel safe and secure. Most situations are now occurring out of fear energy. Pleasant situations usually occur due to a buildup of love energy. In order to distinguish between romantic energy and unconditional love energy I will use the word "acceptance." Unconditional love is very close in energy to acceptance. When you allow people and situations to be part of your life it is due to acceptance of that person or situation. You evaluate, in your mind, as to whether or not a person fits with you and then you allow them in. This is how you create most of what you live with. You judge it as good or okay and then you let it in. This is pretty natural, as you are magnetic in nature and like attracts like.

Once you have "allowed" a person into your life, you then begin to judge their behavior to determine whether or not you will keep them. This is discernment and is taught here on earth as a good habit to embrace. If you decide to keep your new friend, you may begin to find flaws in them that you have not previously noticed. You then begin to push at this person to be more like you think they should be. Here is the problem: all people who come to you are being drawn to you (magnetically) by the energy signals that you are emitting. If you have a victim perspective, you might draw to you those who are more controlling and aggressive. If you have a controlling perspective, you might draw to you those who are more timid and have a victim perspective. It's all energy drawing and repelling. You may not like to hear this and you may not want to believe that you are responsible for drawing certain energy to you, but this is the truth of the matter.

Light energy draws more light to it and dark energy, or denser energy, will draw more of the same to it. This is simple physics and has nothing to do with being a good or bad person. This has to do with the energy that you carry, from the wounds and trauma and even love in your childhood and back into many, many past lives. It's all energy and you, my dear sweet child, are emitting energy!

❧

For the most part you believe that you are a mess. This is due to programming. When you are a small child you are constantly being trained to become a valuable adult. This training requires the use of the word "no." It also requires that you be told whenever you do something wrong. This allows you to grow up with a strong belief in right and wrong. You now have strong programming that tells you, "You do not behave properly." If you experienced strong emotions with your training and guidance, you may have experienced fear at being told how wrong you were in your behavior. You may still carry this fear and it may affect your nervous system, as well as create greater fear whenever you make a mistake or do something wrong.

This is considered programming and you all have this type of programming to one degree or another. Now you may experience these original emotions of fear when you find yourself in a difficult situation, especially when dealing with authority figures such as government, or military, or police, or bosses, or teachers. Even spouses and family who are in a control position may set off an emotional response in you. Any criticism brings up emotional energy and will make you sad or maybe angry. After all, training is considered a critique of your abilities.

Now; I bring up such simple and common examples of emotions to show you how common it is to have fear in you that may affect your behavior in adulthood. This is not just your problem... as a human living with other humans, this has become a worldwide problem. "Fear" is the only problem on earth and "love" is the one and only answer or solution to your problem. So, how do we get from fear to love? The information being given now through many, who have discovered this truth about love, is being shared as more light comes into this dimension. So here is the trick to rising "up" to love: Listen only to the most positive, loving information. Listen to information that is steeped in kindness and understanding.

I realize that you love drama and intrigue and fighting and especially you love being right. However, now is the time to switch to love, kindness and understanding of human behavior and human fear. Fear leads to trauma which leads to hurt feelings which leads to criticism, which then leads to out and out anger. Let it go! Let all anger and criticism go!

Now – this is not a rule nor is it a command. This is simply a suggestion for those of you who wish to drain the energy of fear from your body (your cells and atoms). If you do not care to rise up to love at this time, it is simply a choice. You do no wrong and you never have done anything wrong. Wrongdoing is simply something that man created in order to control his behavior. Wrong is only in the eye of the beholder. Even death is not wrong, you simply move to a new level or dimension. You never ever end, so you never ever really die. We'll discuss death further as we go but, for now, know that you do nothing wrong no matter how many you may have killed in past lives.

Your training has convinced you that you are wrong in certain behaviors and, of course, your neighbors training may have been different than your own, depending on the belief of their trainers. You all go through some type of training if you are human and living on earth. So what sets you off and why do you hate and fear and get angry over things that don't even bother some of your friends? And why do your friends fear and get angry over things that you could care less about? It is all programming. I don't care how right you think you are and how wrong you think they are. It is all programming.

You are learning at this time about "duality" – right/wrong, good/bad. You literally live in a world of duality and you are constantly choosing sides. I want you to stop. In any given debate I would like you to move more to the center. Let go of extreme thinking and move to a calmer position. If you wish to rise above the chaos of duality, you must first move your own energy out of the chaos. What you put your energy into will grow in size. You are a creating machine. You create with your energy. Thoughts carry energy. Where are you pointing your thoughts? Where is your focus aimed? Where are you going? You move yourself into realities and out of realities. Where are you moving you now?

❧

You will find that the most difficult part of rising up is letting go. You wish to hold on to your idea, and your belief, that you are morally right and everyone who does not agree with your perspective on life is morally off base.

So, the best thing to do is to start from scratch. Pretend like you do not have an opinion. Pretend like both sides of any argument have a valid point. Pretend to be a non participant observer of life on this planet. Let go of judgment and criticism and evaluation of life in general, especially if you see life as terrible at this time. Life is not terrible, and most situations occur due to evolution and change. In the same way that you see destruction when something new is being created, you will see destruction and a tearing down of the old in order to make room for the new. You cannot build a new building on top of an old building.

Do not be so quick to judge the reconstruction that you see going on around you. Energy is constantly going out from spirit beings and this energy is creative in nature. This causes matter and the material world to constantly shift and change. These spirits inhabit bodies and are called humans. You are constantly creating by emitting energy. You may create new beautiful and kind situations by emitting new beautiful and kind energy. You get to change the world by adding to it in a beautiful way. Simply let go of the old way of judging and criticizing. Put more kindness and love and generosity into your creations. Begin by letting go of your need to hold on to your moral judgments. You have been trained to judge and to condemn, and it is time now to rise above the old traditions and beliefs that lead you to believe in a punishing God. This has created many problems for you and is a good place to start with your new letting go process.

First things first – God does not judge you or anyone else. I don't care how big the crime is in your eyes – God does not judge you or anyone else, not ever! Second – you are God energy. You literally come from God and are made of the same stuff that you come from. Get these two things straight in your mind and you will make a turn in your belief system towards a higher direction. The key here is to get you to turn around. You have been headed in one direction and now it is time to move in the opposite direction. Go up! Rise above all the silliness and name calling and criticism and misunderstanding of creation. You are totally unaware and you are fighting with your own self. You are all from the same source, the same God stuff makes you all up. You are so unconscious that you have forgotten who and what you are. You have even forgotten why you came and who you came into this dimension with. This is a grand awakening and you are right on schedule to wake up and become aware and conscious.

These are wonderful times and the construction of something new is well on its way. You are moving into a new awareness and a new dimension of thought. Thought is the energy that drives you and has the ability to move you in this direction or that direction. Do you see the world as in danger and going to hell in a hand basket, or do you see the world as simply changing and growing in a new direction? You get to decide how you see everything by what you choose to focus on. Make it good. Make it kind. Make it beautiful!

*W*hen you begin to see how you have always wanted to do the right thing in order to receive approval, you begin to realize how you might be judging yourself for your behavior. You wish to love you and to nurture you and this has not necessarily been programmed into you. You have grown up with the programming that you were trained with. This programming may tell you that you require some sort of punishment for wrong behavior. If this is the case, you may feel the need to punish yourself whenever you do something wrong or make a mistake. This punishment may be as simple as feeling down or sad for a while. It may also be as complex as having a fall or hurting yourself while exercising. This is common among you and you usually do not realize that you are dealing with self-punishment.

So now we have you with some type of injury, maybe big or small, and you feel worse about life in general. The predominant thought may be "why is this always happening to me," or in case of religious beliefs, "why is God punishing me?" God does not punish you ever! In the case of self-punishment, God can only watch and hope that you wake up to what is really going on. Everything, absolutely everything, is cause and effect. Thoughts that say, "I am bad" or "I did something wrong," often pile up and create strong energy stores within the billions and trillions of atoms and cells of your body. You then walk around, as an energy being, affecting all other energy that you come into contact with. And since everything is energy, you literally interact with and affect all other energy.

You are in an interactive universe. Everything here is cause and effect. You are moving in accordance with the energy that you are, and some of it has been so strongly programmed into you that you are being moved in a direction you do not wish to go. You are constantly reprogramming yourself with your thoughts. Whenever you think "I am good, I am love," you move you in a new direction. When you think "life is good, life is love," you move you in a new direction. Whenever you think "he is good" or "she is good," you move you in a new direction. And when you think "he is awful or terrible," you may as well have thought "I am awful, I am terrible," simply because you just ran that energy through your body – your cells and your atoms. You then emit awful and terrible energy into the atmosphere to affect all life in this dimension. And the more awful and terrible energy that is emitted, it becomes like pollution that affects everything and all other energy.

If enough of you put out enough hate it will begin to affect you all and because you are all made of energy, you may reverse this trend. You may think how wonderful life is and how wonderful it is to be in human form and how good you can feel at moments. And the more you emit these positive thoughts the greater you, and the cells in your body, will grow with this positive, healing, uplifting energy. The more you lighten your load of energy in this way, the less stress on all the cells of your body, simply because they will no longer be carrying the heavy weight of the denser energy. Your body will no longer be fighting this gravity pull and will be allowed to vibrate faster and to feel lighter, and it will become easier for your immune system to do its work and heal you.

You may heal you simply by changing your programming. Make it lighter. Give up the addiction to judgment and putdowns. Begin to see everything as having a purpose and then do not judge and condemn. No awful, no terrible! Just peace and love and kindness and understanding. You can do this! You are a creating machine! Begin to create what you want, not what you don't want!

$\mathscr{I}$ hope you find what you're looking for! What do you spend the majority of your time thinking about or focusing on? Do you find that you spend your day focusing on the gifts of life? Maybe the beautiful trees in your neighborhood or maybe the bright colored leaves or flowers in bloom. Do you see the beauty in the sky above and in the formation of white fluffy clouds? Do you enjoy going to a park and observing nature? These are ways of placing your energy "in" beauty and away from scenes that you may not enjoy.

Spend as much time as possible looking for, and at, those things that bring you pleasure. This will assist in shifting your energy up to a faster, lighter vibration. The idea is to get as much of the denser, heavier vibrations out of you as possible. We want you light as a feather in order to move up to the higher dimensions of love and peace. You will find that you can make this shift fairly easily if you don't spend time and energy focusing on the negatives.

When negative thoughts pop into your head simply catch yourself and switch to something lighter and more positive. It may help to have a favorite tree to look at or maybe a favorite statue or painting... anything that is pleasing to you and will assist you in rising up. Once you get the hang of this it will become quite easy to raise your spirits. Your spirits are basically your inner life. When your inner life is down, you tend to go down with it. This is due to emotional energy, and emotional energy can be quite strong. Sometimes you must allow the emotions to drain in a healthy way. Emotional energy is simply trapped energy from previous trauma. This can be quite difficult to deal with, and it will help you to know that all emotional energy from past trauma is easily cleared and released from the body once you face the fear of the original trauma. I have written an entire series of books through Liane explaining the ins and outs of healing and clearing energy. If you have past trauma you may wish to take a look at this series. I won't go into clearing and releasing energy here in detail, but know that the information is available in *the Loving Light Books series.*

Now, when you begin to release past trauma, you will be giving yourself a very big gift. Any time you let go of something you have been holding on to, you naturally and automatically become lighter. It's pretty simple really – light, happy thoughts in, make you light and happy – heavy, angry thoughts in, make you heavy and angry. It's sort of like "you are what you eat" only this is more "you are what you think."

So; how do we keep you happy and light? We guide you to the center. We come out of duality and you will automatically begin to lift and feel better. Struggle is at the extreme edges. Draw a circle and make a line straight through the center. This is you. Now, on one end of the line write the word "fear." On the other end of the line write the word "love." Where do you sit on this line? Whenever a situation or even a topic of discussion comes up, I want you to move to the center. If you are at the fear end you must move closer to love. If you are at the love side move to the center so you do not disappear from earth. I'm just kidding – if you were at the extreme side of love you would be vibrating so fast that you would not be visible here on earth. You would be God once again. So, needless to say, no one on earth, at this time, is at the extreme side of love which is total unconditional acceptance.

Use your circle to measure where you are on any topic that may come up in conversation. Do you go to the center and not fight for one side or the other? Probably not. This is not how you were trained. You were trained to fight for your rights and to take a stand. This worked for you at one time, but now times have changed and you are no longer feeding the ego, you are beginning to feed the soul. The ego loves winning, being on top, having more, being better than others, competition and did I say winning? Oh yes, we "love" to be right and smart and winning. This is the job of the ego and it does its job well. Now we are moving out of the ego and in spirit. We are literally journeying into our soul, our very own God self.

This is for those of you who are on that journey now. This book is not an instruction manual on how to be good and right in your behavior. This information is being given for those who wish to rise above the struggle and chaos of duality. This information is for those who are not afraid to drop out of the rules that govern fear and move over to the acceptance and tolerance that are part of unconditional love. It can be a very scary thing to let go of fear and move into acceptance of life and to flow with life, but the rewards are very great indeed.

≈≈≈

For as long as you can remember, you have been light. You feel like you are human and emotion and thought, but you are really a light being who inhabits form. Once you remember who you really are, it will be easier for you to connect with that part of you.

You will find that you are no longer so stressed once you let go of the idea that you must be perfect. You went through a great deal of training in childhood and this training has had some unintended effects. You often find fault with yourself and with your own behavior. This leads to even greater unintended results such as low self-esteem and low self-worth. Here is the truth of the matter: You are a beautiful soul! You are a soul who is on an adventure. You are a soul who has chosen to be the one and only you. You are a soul who decided to experience situations that would move the light being energy that makes up a soul, into the most effective position for growth. Each soul who comes to earth has a purpose or idea of how it wishes to express through matter. Each soul sets up a path that will lead to the best expression of energy that will lead to the soul's final destination, or complete its journey into matter in the most beneficial way. Souls are expressing and playing in matter in the same way that you might play and express yourself in a song or a painting.

You do no wrong when you use your creative expression and capabilities. You are simply a part of God who is expressing through matter and being creative. You may make as many mistakes as you like because there really are no mistakes. No brushstroke that you make is ever wrong or a mistake. There are many trained artists who will tell you that this stroke or that idea is wrong, but they are simply following their strong training and programming. The first artist had no training and was totally free to express without fear of harsh criticism or judgment.

You are an artist and you are allowing your training to make you feel guilty. You want to control others, and so you may choose to make them feel guilty about their choices and their behavior or way of creating. All this manipulation and control of your own creative abilities, and those of others, is causing problems for you now. So remember – there is no right or wrong way for a soul, who lives forever and never ends, to create or express through matter. It is all a matter of free will and choice. Everything is simply cause and effect.

So, what do you choose as an effect and what will be the cause of that effect. Choose the thoughts, ideas and movements (or even non-action) that will give you your desired effect. Do you want love and understanding – give out love and understanding. Do you want peace and calm – give out peace and calm. Let go of your desire to get involved with chaotic, argumentative energy if you choose to live in peaceful, calm energy.

We all have our creations to deal with but once we "choose" to change direction, not out of guilt that we are doing wrong but out of wanting to rise up in vibration, we will let go of some of that guilt, and our bodies will relax and our cells will feel lighter, and our low self-esteem will begin to drain out of us. We will then be free to receive "self-love." We will become who we truly are. We will have found our true self.

As you continue to grow in awareness, you will continue to speed up your vibration. As you speed up in vibration, you give off a lighter energy. As you give off lighter energies, you will attract lighter energy to you. Light energy emitted equals light energy received. This is pretty easy to understand and would really be all you need to understand. So light in equals light out which draws more light to you. This is fun isn't it? It's good to know that "you" control it all and how easily you might do so. Light out draws more light! Think of this all day today as you go to work or play. "Light energy out draws more light energy into my life."

God

⚜

*F*or the most part you do not believe that you are God. You think of God mostly as a punishing ruler. This is what western religion has taught. Even some eastern religions teach that God punishes and rewards. This is not the truth of the situation. I have written a book titled *For the Love of God: an introduction to God.* This book will help guide you away from any belief that you may carry regarding God as a ruler and a punisher of men and women. God does not ever punish anyone, not even your enemies. So please let go of such nonsense.

God creates and God is white light energy. The only part of God who punishes is the part that is inhabiting man and trying to get man's ego to let go of its hold on you. So, God does not punish, however God accepts all as it is. This is due to the fact that nothing is bad and nothing is wrong once you come out of duality. Once you come to the center, it will become easier for you to simply "observe" life and no longer judge life. You will be free of the illusion. You will rise above the illusion and know that everything that you see on earth is part of a giant play that souls are acting out.

Souls come in groups, sometimes large groups, to enjoy this huge playground. You may have come into this life with many soul friends. Souls are made of energy and so there is no fencing them in. They come and go and inhabit many forms. They move in waves and they float and flow and play and observe. They are aware of your fears and your desires. They guide you through intuition and feelings, and they try their best to contact you and to have communication and relationship with you. This is done on spiritual levels as well as human levels. Souls are always happy to be part of this game that you play. Your soul is you! It is the most real part of you and it has experienced a great many lifetime roles with you. You simply

34

don a costume and you become a character and you act in accordance to the role you, as soul, planned to be.

So, what was your plan? What role did you choose? And "if" there is no right or wrong in reality, did you do all that you planned on accomplishing? If not, is that a problem? No – nothing is really a problem. Did you wish to do more or rise higher in your awareness of the illusion? If not – no problem – it's all good! "Don't worry, be happy" is a very good motto to live by. You are right where you wanted to be or you would not be here. You may change direction any time you wish and you may grow in greater awareness any time you wish. You get to choose where you wish to go and you get to choose how high you wish to rise up out of this illusion. It's all just a game that eternal, never-ending spirits play. Don't be angry or feel deceived. On some level you already know all of this and you, God you/soul you, are the one who put the plan into motion.

You have a great deal to learn about your own God self. The good news is that the more aware you become of this part of yourself the bigger it will grow. Remember, you are a creating machine and you emit energy that will grow bigger where ever it is placed.

⚛

For the most part, you do not believe that you are good. You believe in bad and wrongdoing so strongly that your belief is taking over and making you sad and depressed. You have turned to drugs and medications because you do not realize that your perspective on life is really the problem. You spend your life judging and criticizing and watching for things that go wrong. You require balance of thought! You require a reset of your mind and this will allow your emotional body to calm down, which in turn will allow your physical and mental bodies to heal.

So this is what I wish you to do... I wish you to take today off from worry and careful thinking. I wish you to be free and not listen to any stressful conversations. I wish you to take a vacation from any sort of negativity and simply "be." Be you, the spirit/soul you that you truly are. Be peaceful, be calm, be happy and know that you are wonderful just as you are. Do not find anything wrong with anything you see. Everything that you see will serve a purpose; you just are unaware of that purpose.

Say you see two people fighting and arguing. Then one of them punches the other and knocks him to the ground. Do not judge this situation. In other words, do not get all emotionally upset and certainly do not interfere. Let two spirits, who came to earth to have a good fight (or boxing match), play this game that they came to play. On this day, when you are taking a break from judgment, you will see how these two souls are actually good friends; and because it is impossible to fight or push each other around when one does not have a body, spirits come to this place where they can enjoy physical expression. No right, no wrong... simply spirit expressing through matter. If you were/are a spirit, wouldn't you enjoy some physical movement and expression once you don a suit that allows you this freedom of expression – especially if you know who you are and how you never ever end or die? You simply spend your never-ending existence playing in the various dimensions because it's fun. It is fun to act out a role in a play or movie where you are simply pretending.

The next step in your evolution is to rise above the illusion of this game that you all are playing. Today will be a practice day for you to see how life can be in the higher dimensions of love (acceptance).

☙❧

So far you have done well. You came from God/spirit energy and you entered matter. You, soul you, began a life in this third dimension without a guidebook on how to operate a physical body. You entered form after requesting to do so. You usually request a soul friend to be the host body for you. Sometimes you make agreements based on the host soul requesting that you come into their body to share their life. They, the soul host, may be a very old friend who has shared many lifetimes with you and simply enjoys having you in their life once again.

When you send out a request for a soul friend to host you, it may be in exchange for a request on their part. Say you have a soul who wants to experience growth in a specific area. Maybe this soul wishes to learn unconditional love, or maybe this soul wants to learn how to grow beyond trauma and suffering. This soul may go into agreement with other soul friends who say, "Fine, I'll help you with your path if you help me with mine." Maybe a soul wants to learn to overcome fear of anger while in a physical body. As a soul there is no fear, as nothing is dangerous or harmful, and souls do not experience emotions without a physical body. A soul is simply white light (aware) energy that has come from God Source.

So we have this soul who wishes to "experience anger" so that he/she might figure out how to overcome anger while in physical form. The best way to teach yourself how to swim is to jump in the water. The best way to teach yourself how to rise above anger is to jump into an angry environment. So – many souls set up agreements in order to learn and grow and more efficiently operate a physical body which contains mind and emotions.

We now have an agreement whereby a tiny new baby ends up in an angry environment. Why? Simply because a soul is playing with matter and learning how to use matter to express. In this case, the soul wishes to overcome fear of anger while still unconscious of the fact that he/she is God consciousness. The host soul, because she is a friend, grants the request of the incoming soul and may add a stipulation such as, "If I bring you in and show you my anger, will you forgive me before you leave earth this lifetime?" Forgiveness is very important on a soul level, as souls never judge or hold grudges. Souls simply observe. The host soul is asking for forgiveness because it knows that judgment is heavy and dense and will affect the younger body if it is not released.

Souls work together in many ways and on many projects. Things that look like fighting and arguing may be something else altogether. It may simply be two spirits learning how to live in a body in a healthier way – without fear of anger or perhaps without fear of some other behavior. I just thought you would like to know that perspective is everything and you may wish to see things from a higher view.

"Remember – from a soul perspective this is all fun and games and play. It's an illusion… a game."

God

✾

*B*efore you can raise your vibration you must become more of what you truly are. You are soul. You are spirit. You are God. You are eternal, never-ending, always-changing, white light energy. You produce energy and you emit energy. You shift and you change with every thought. Your thoughts become beliefs and your beliefs become who you are. You literally live in your beliefs and they surround you and they affect you and they definitely affect your emotions.

Your emotional body is part of you and it moves. Your emotions pull you with them. They may go up or down and you tend to go up or down with them. Now – emotions are a tricky subject because you can suppress them just as you would, or might, suppress a thought. Emotions tend to affect you more strongly than you realize, and since they do affect you so strongly you may tend to use them as a guide. If you feel down, you may think denser or heavier thoughts. This thought energy then goes out from you and draws more dense and heavy energy to you. More dense heavy thought energy creates, or stimulates, greater dense and heavy emotions.

So, here's the trick to removing yourself from dense energy: Once you feel strong, heavy emotions surface, allow them to come to the surface and to release. Then do not act them out! Simply observe them and tell yourself that this is actually a good thing. You are releasing heaviness that has held you down, so that you now may rise up to the dimensions of love and light. Dense emotions tend to draw dense thoughts and thought patterns. Allow them to rise to the surface of your awareness and use this observing technique to release them without creating greater turmoil in your personal reality.

Remember – you get to live in the energy that you emit around you. You may lighten your personal reality by allowing energy to come to the surface and not judge it. Allow, accept, observe and do not judge.

When you feel dense emotions come up consider asking yourself, "What am I releasing? What am I clearing?" Then remind yourself that it is a good thing to get the weightier energies up and out if your goal is to rise above the denseness of this planet. Earth is surrounded with, and by, energy that is being emitted every day by its inhabitants. You have the power to rise "above" all negative thought, by simply letting go of your addiction to the drama of this world and focusing on the comedy and love and kindness that is all around you. "There's not much comedy and love and kindness" – you shout! I wonder what you are focusing on? Look away and look for the good! It is there. It is always there. Find a point of light and move your focus in that direction. Find one person who you see as good and kind and then find another and another.

In the same way that you have led yourself down into judgment, you may draw yourself back up to acceptance. You do not like the word acceptance and you are afraid to allow everything to just "be." You fear being hurt and so you try to control everything. This is understandable since you were, and still are, being programmed and trained to fear. Come over to love! It takes a little courage and you must begin to let go of your constant need for drama, but I have great faith that you can come out of this hole you have created. You will rise up to see the beauty and the greatness of your life. You will begin to love and accept you once again. The more you judge you, the lower into your hole you go. Do not judge! Love and accept!

Run the energy of acceptance through your emotional and mental bodies by running the energy of acceptance through "you"... physical you. The cells and atoms of your body are affected by every thought that you think, simply because they are made up of energy, and thoughts are energy and energy moves and changes energy. You are a thinking, creating machine. You create your world view and then you live in it. How is your picture of life looking right now? Is it magical and childlike, or is it cluttered with years of dense energy that just needs to be released? You control your perspective of life. Let it be good and happy and light.

❧

For the most part you are afraid. You are afraid of death. You are afraid of life and you are afraid of loss. Your biggest fear is pain. Whether emotional or physical, pain is a big concern. This is how to overcome pain... allow it to sit with you a little at a time. Pain is a signal that tells you to look and listen. Some part of your body, maybe your nervous system or your emotions, are sending a signal that says, "Something is wrong here and needs to be a attended to." You do not like pain and will avoid it at all costs.

Since pain is part of existing in this three dimensional world, it will be helpful to you to know that you may calm your pain by calming your emotions and thoughts. Try this – the next time you have a headache or stub your toe begin to relax and soothe yourself. Allow your emotional body to stay calm and breathe. Tell yourself that everything will be okay and pretend that you are nurturing a small child. The more you can send love to yourself the less the pain signal will be. Pain signals are meant to protect you from harming yourself further. You actually used a system of self-awareness when you were primitive and it was part of your nature to understand your body and its signals. You have grown so far away from intuition that you no longer understand your own body and its signals to you.

So if you can become more connected to yourself, your body will no longer feel the need to send such strong signals and your pain will lesson. Even emotional pain will lessen once you are fully listening to and nurturing you. If you have adopted the motto, "No pain no gain" your body will follow your instructions. It is best to believe in "painless gain" and this will assist you in many ways. Going with the flow of your life and not fighting life at every turn, allows you to flow through life without the fighting and struggle that you have become so accustomed to. It is all you, creating as you go. Flow with life and life will flow for you.

When you let go of your desire to pop a pill for every little thing, your body will cease to send such strong signals. After all, you only need to yell if someone is not listening and paying attention. Begin to pay attention to what you think and what you tell yourself. If you think you are awful that is called criticism of self. Self-criticism will lead to pain. Why? Simply because your thoughts and beliefs build up inside your body. Every thought you think is energy running through your body and this energy affects anything it touches. So, what is inside of your body? Billions and trillions of cells and atoms. And what are these billions and trillions of atoms and cells made of? Energy! You are an energy being. You are living energy, and when awful feelings or criticism passes from your mind it moves through your entire body and affects all of you. You then wonder why you have a headache and you want to shut it off so you take a pill.

I am not saying that taking a pill is bad; I am only giving you cause and effect ideas to show you another way. You might begin to listen to your headache signal and ask to be shown how to communicate with yourself. Lack of communication causes stronger signals to be sent that are basically saying, "Stop all this criticism, please." Once you stop all criticism your mind will begin to let go of some of the old criticism energy that is stored there, and change can begin to take place. Criticism is very popular among you, and you love to give your honest opinion which is based on all that training and programming that you carry.

Begin to let go of everything that does not serve you. This includes ideas, thoughts, attitudes and beliefs. Stop jumping up and shouting your opinion until you know, or become fully aware of, exactly how your opinion was created and how it may cause greater problems for you. Pain is caused by emotions as well as physical injury. Pain may be healed by emotions as well as physical nurturing. Do not be so quick to get rid of physical pain, as it may be telling you something important that can assist you in the way you love or do not love yourself. Self-love and self-understanding is very important in your existence, and yet you spend little to no time understanding your body and your emotions and, most importantly, your energy thoughts that affect your energy level and your physical and emotional and mental bodies. Love you! Listen to you! Nurture you! Do not bombard "you" with negative energy whether it is directed at you or directed at the bad guy in the movie you are watching. Come away from criticism, at least until you can unload some of your excess storage. You are drowning in criticism and it is taking you down with it.

৵৶

You have been human many, many times. You have been soul/spirit/God forever.

You will begin to discover that you operate from your human/ego/fear side and rarely do you allow spirit/soul/God to intervene. This is about to change for many of you. You are going to become aware of the fact that you are a soul, who is in matter and learning to control matter by simply taking the wheel and driving. You are learning about soul energy in an effort to rise above the struggle of human life by creating peace, love and joy.

Do your constant arguments and debates and being right bring you great peace? Are you headed in the direction you wish to go? Do you feel at peace and happy when you focus on negative thoughts, worries and concerns? Can you let go of being right long enough to be love? Will you ever rise above your ego self and move into soul self?

You will find that the more light, positive, loving information that you take in, the greater your chance of moving up and rising above the drama, chaos and duality. It is actually possible to not get sucked into the drama and lessons of others. Sometimes what you see as an atrocity is not. Sometimes what you see as dangerous is not, and sometimes what you see as hatred is only fear being acted out. So, begin to open your psyche to trust. Begin to allow a little trust in your soul and its ways. Allow yourself to not get involved. I know that you are taught and trained to stand up and fight to protect your rights and your country, but you are at a juncture right now and it is important for you to surrender to your soul. Your God self is in you and growing and you are rising above duality. It is impossible to rise above something if you are busy defending it.

For right now it is best to surrender to love and kindness and understanding and peace. Give up the fight! Give up the fight for right now. If, after you have love, peace and harmony, you prefer to go back to fighting and arguing and pursuing your rights, you may do so. You have free will. You have always had free will and you will always be a free spirit-being living within a human form. You get to direct the body and mind and emotions. Allow your soul, your spirit, your higher self to take over and let go of trying to control everything. Allow life to unfold and focus on the magic and the beauty. You create with your thoughts. Are you putting more thought energy into being right or is your energy, your power, your fuel for creating, going into negative outcomes? Put your power into peace and you will see peace. Put your power into fighting and you will see war. The choice is yours… it has always been yours.

⁂

$\mathcal{S}$o far you have been receptive to most of the information given here. You realize that you may be much more than simply a human who is walking this planet.

You will begin to discover many new assets in being a soul who is aware and can guide your body and mind. When you turn to soul guidance, you are literally turning in towards your own God self. Most of you do not hear from your own God self, simply because there is a great deal blocking the communication lines inward. Some of you set it up in advance to communicate directly with soul or spirit energy, in an effort to fulfill a goal or project. This goal may have been to bring light energy into this dimension, or it may have been to help raise you up, or it may have been to raise others up.

It's not a problem if you do not hear directly from God/spirit energy. It is not a problem if you do not raise your vibration. It is not a problem if you stay right where you are and continue to experience life as you always have. This is free will and freedom of choice which is available to all. So please do not push at your friends and your family and your neighbors to change simply because you have a desire to rise up and to see all of humanity rise up.

Raising awareness is a very lofty goal and is best entered into with kindness, love and empathy. No one should be expected to see life as you see life. You are each layered with your own life experiences, as well as all those past life experiences, and you do not project your perspective onto others. You do not want to bully and to be so arrogant as to believe that your way is the right way! There is no right way. There are plans and goals and free will choices that may have been set in place long before entering this life. You may not force your life goals and your rules for behavior onto another. It is simply not a way to rise above and become aware – if that is your goal.

When you push at others to change, you are pushing energy at them. When you push energy at an energy being, you are basically pushing them away from you. In addition, you are saying, "I do not like you, so please change in order for me to accept you." This will, of course, work with those who are vulnerable but may backfire on you at some point. When you blame someone for the way they behave, you are actually blaming you. Why? Simply because the energy that says, "I blame you, you are not acceptable the way you are" is now running through your body and your cells and your atoms. The person you blame does not receive this (heavy) blame energy unless they believe you and take it in. We would then have two of you who are now walking around carrying dense, heavy energy.

So – the key to happiness and to lightening your load is acceptance. Acceptance allows you to overcome your fears which keep you from love. Acceptance frightens you because it is "trust." You do not like trust because you were trained and programmed to not trust anyone or anything. Trust will lift you up and trust will allow you to free yourself of judgment and guilt. You must begin to trust if you wish to rise higher. This is not a rule and it is not a command. I am simply relaying cause and effect information here. Trust will free you from your anchor, your weight that is holding you down. Trust God. Trust your soul to guide you and trust life. Trust that you can overcome any issues that may arise and trust that "love" is always the answer!

*You have been on this discovery journey since you entered earth. If your soul plan was to enter earth and, while in the dense energy of matter, remember that you are part of God, you are on your way to your goal.

You have been waking up your entire life. In order for a soul to enter a body, the soul must go unconscious. It is similar to diving under water; you must wear a diving suit and mask that is appropriate for the depth you intend to go. Then, after you acclimate and learn a few breathing techniques, you may begin to awaken to the truth of your identity. Many of you communicated with your soul, or what you call guides, in your long ago past. At one point in history it was common knowledge that humans and spirits communicated freely. Now it is considered paranormal and uncommon. It is even considered strange and weird. For those who are very religious, it may be considered blasphemy if they believe that God/soul/spirit does not communicate with those they inhabit.

It's strange when you think about it... how can a spirit, or soul, that is part of God, come to earth and dwell in a human form, or body, that never wishes to communicate with it? Why would a soul take on this task if it knows that it will be shunned and ignored? What is the purpose of such a journey? Maybe, just maybe, it's fun to try. Maybe everything isn't so serious as you humans make it out to be. Maybe this is a time for reconnecting with your own higher self, and maybe that is why you are reading a book titled *Journey into Your Soul.* Maybe you are already beginning to wake up to the fact that you are soul energy come from God. Maybe you are letting go of your fear of self, your fear that you are God. After all, the fear of God has been taught here on earth for eons and it literally teaches you to fear part of yourself.

Is that any way to live? Can you imagine growing up in a home where you literally fear your parents and must control your fear at all times? Then imagine if you live inside of a body that fears you and fears being you. How would you respond (soul/spirit you) if you knew that you were so feared by the person you dwell within? How would you gradually and gently make your human aware of yourself? Would you yell at them to "wake up and remember" that they come from God, or would you gently and lovingly guide them to information that would assist them in waking up to their true identity?

Your soul sits in you and guides you and allows you to be whomever and however you wish to be. Your soul does not come forward because of your level, or degree, of fear. When you begin to ask and to trust, your soul will begin to merge with you and you will more easily communicate with that part of you. The choice is yours. Your soul will not bust down your door to greet you. Your soul has ultimate love and acceptance for all that you do. Your soul will gently guide you until you are ready to open the door of communication by asking or inviting soul to come forward.

"You have a friend in you!" Literally – you have a friend "in" you.

❧

*W*hen you begin to realize how you are creative in ways you do not yet acknowledge, you will wish to learn how to direct your creative energies in a way that may assist you in your personal endeavors. You may wish to create wealth and health and happiness.

The easiest way to create happiness is to stop judging yourself and your circumstances. You judge yourself out of habit and you will wish to redirect this energy. You will wish to use this energy to praise yourself. I realize that you have been taught to be humble and only praise others, but this is a change in direction. You will not become vain and arrogant. You will begin to like how it feels to be praised and you will begin to change your beliefs and your feeling toward yourself. You are both lovable and praiseworthy. Do not take this lightly, as it will be very helpful in your rise up.

Once we get you to praise yourself you will feel more comfortable when others praise you. You will also let go of your desire to tear others down. You will let go of your need to find villains and bad guys. You will learn to focus on those you admire, rather than those you hate or judge as unworthy. One of your biggest issues is finding fault with others. You have been strongly programmed to look for the bad guys, the tricksters, the scammers, the villains of life. You hate bullies and you hate anyone who is unkind. It is time now to turn the other cheek and walk away. Turn your focus away! What you focus on, you send your thoughts to. What you send your thoughts to will grow, simply because thoughts "are" energy. It is like blowing up a balloon. What you put your breath into gets bigger. So please stop talking about your enemies and your perceived villains. Let the bad guys live in their own dimension and move yourself up to the next highest level of awareness. You may choose to "live and let live" and you will be assisting yourself in a very big way.

I realize that fear of being harmed and fear of loss is very big and blown out of proportion for many of you, but it is time now to release fear and move over to the love side of things. Love will come through once you let go of fear. Trust in life and trust in a higher power will help you release your very strong grip on fear of life in general. It is most difficult to be happy in life when you are so busy fearing it and all those who live life with you. When you judge them as bad, you judge you as bad. The thought energy running through your body and your cells and your atoms is "you are bad." How can you possibly be happy when you are being bombarded with "you are bad," or, "you do not deserve," or, "you need to be punished?"

Please watch how you use your creative abilities. Learn to praise you and to praise life. If your friends and family do not wish to hear the positive side of things, do not force it on them. "Live and let live." Go with the flow of where you are being guided by your soul, and allow them their free will choice of staying right where they are. Treat it as you would a small vulnerable child or toddler. You would not expect a toddler to understand the complexities of life and you would not force your political or religious fears on a small toddler... or would you?

Learn to let go and let God take care of worldly concerns. I realize you just want to help the good guys win, but you do not understand energy and dimensions and how you move within them. Please, if you wish to be happy, let go of your need to be right. It is okay to be helpful, it becomes a problem when you begin to control. It is not really a problem, as there are no problems, but I must work within your understanding of language. I am guiding you, in this book (and the others I have channeled through Liane), to understand energy and cause and effect. No right or wrong, no good or bad, only cause and effect, e.g., you throw a rock in a pond and it creates a ripple effect. Cause and effect is where you are in your learning.

I have written a book titled *Your Return to the Light of Love* and it will be most helpful for you to read if you wish to learn how to let go of judgment. For now I will ask you to please begin to be aware of how you judge you by judging others. You will wish to turn the other cheek and begin to praise you in the process.

❧

*A*s far as I can tell, you are still me. You are still the energy of light that moved into a very dense part of existence. You are part of God, or your Source, that has moved out or expanded from your core. You have not left God or your Source. You are only moving in an outward direction and now it is time to wake up and focus on your true identity.

Your true identity is one of light. Your true identity is one of total awareness and acceptance that you contain absolutely everything. You are everything and everything is you. You contain all information and expression and knowledge and possibilities that have ever, or will ever exist. It is all you.

You came from the Source and you have the ability to shift and to change into anything that you can imagine and it will be done. Do you dream when you sleep, and when you dream do you literally feel like you are part of your dream? This is what is occurring now. You are dreaming, and you think your dream is the real you simply because you are in the middle of it. This is not the real you. You are dreaming and I am trying to gently and kindly rouse you from sleep. You have gone to sleep is all... you have dozed off and are living in a dream reality that is an illusion.

I am waking you now because your dream is scaring you. Your dream has become frightening for you and you are literally screaming and praying and, in some cases, begging for assistance. I am here at your request. God, the Light Source, the awareness of All That Is, is trying to get your attention and calm your fears, as they are causing you stress and the resulting stress is causing you more of the same. You are magnetic in nature and you will draw to you exactly what you contain. Right now you contain a great deal of fear energy. The answer to your fear is love. Love is always the answer for you.

You may fight me on this and yell how you require greater protection, however, you are greatly mistaken. What you require right now is love and kindness and nurturing. You cannot be kind and loving and nurturing when you are constantly filling your mind and your body with fearful, angry thoughts. Fill your body and your mind with love and kind thoughts. Loving, kind thoughts will raise you above the energy of fear. Loving, kind thoughts will heal you. Loving, kind thoughts will bring you back to Source, your Source. Loving, kind thoughts will bring you home to you.

You do not require greater protection and greater awareness about what you believe to be wrong with the world. What you do require is greater pleasure and greater awareness of how good life on earth can be for everyone, once love is put in place. It only takes "one" to get the ball rolling. One soul, who has come awake and left the illusion of the dream, can have a great effect on all other sleeping souls. Why? Simply because you are all connected energetically. You are all one giant soul that is immersing itself into unconsciousness in order to play the game of "let's dream up a world and then go into that world and pretend to be a character and act out that character for a while." You are not the character that you pretend to be. You are the master manipulator who is expressing through your character.

⊱⊰

For the first time you are beginning to see how you may be a spirit who is inhabiting a body and not just a human who is stumbling around in the dark.

When you begin to focus on the soul/spirit you, you begin to move in that direction. You literally begin to move over to the God/love side of you and away from the fear side that has been leading you into anger and frustration and exhaustion. Fear can be very draining and love can be very energizing. You will find that the greater your fear, the greater your inflexibility. You will become more flexible with love and less rigid in your belief regarding right and wrong. You will move closer to your center and your life will become one of balance and harmony. You will still have situations to overcome, but they will feel less traumatic and you will move through them with ease. You will become content with life and you will lose your edge. You will soften and you will flow with life and with the circumstances in your life.

Life will become more joyful and you will enjoy your life right where you are. There will be no great struggle to do more and to be more. You will accept you just as you are and this will allow you to accept others just as they are. This does not mean that you will accept murderers and rapists just as they are. This means that you will no longer hold harsh feelings about them. You no longer will view them as villains and evil. You will have greater awareness and this will allow you to let go of your judgment against them. You will rise up in awareness and observation regarding human nature, and in your wisdom you will "realize" how the unfortunate ones have been traumatized to such a level of fear and pain that they are acting on impulse rather than behaving normally.

Normal behavior allows you to flow more readily with life and abnormal behavior is usually caused by great increase in pain. Pain is a signal that can send some people over the edge and they act accordingly. When you are in great pain, it is difficult to contain yourself and to feel empathy for others. You only feel your hurt and you wish to relieve it. This is what occurs with many who are now in your prisons. It is cause and effect. Everything in this three dimensional reality is cause and effect. When you move away from your own fear, you will see how those you now judge as villains are victims of specific behavior and sometimes violence that was acted out on them. There really are no bad guys here. Everyone is only what you make them out to be in your own mind. I would like to see you "lighten" your thinking a bit and give your thoughts a much needed break.

When you constantly look for, and focus on, those you judge as bad and awful, you are constantly sending bad and awful energy through you. You receive what you send. You are the recipient of your thoughts and your beliefs and your own energy. You send your energy through you daily. You send your energy out into the world daily. You surround yourself with your personal reality bubble and you live in it. You literally live "in" the energy of your thoughts and your beliefs. You may choose a lighter reality to live in by accepting that you do not have a clear view of what is really going on.

What is really going on is a movie, a play, none of it is real. It is being created by you as you go and it, your movie, your personal reality, may have a happy, peaceful and harmonious finale or it may not. It is up to you how far towards love you wish to move. Love and understanding are great big gifts. You may use yours or continue to reject these gifts. You get to create romance or comedy or drama; even horror and science fiction are available to you as you create your life movie. There is no right way to go. All ways lead you back to your Source, simply because you have not left your Source. You are only sleeping and dreaming. None of this is real, so please do not feel guilty about lightening up your thoughts and moving over to love and acceptance. See the magic that comes from knowing the secret.

This secret is that this is an illusion, and all the players are really souls who are part of God and are therefore never-ending light energy. They, and you, come here to play act and to be a character and to enjoy the fun of pretending.

So, in order to assist yourself and enjoy this thing called life, it would help if you can just "live and let live" for a while. Once you get the hang of that, you can move on to acceptance, which will lead you home to love. Why love? Simply because love is your true nature. Love is what you are. You may begin to move closer to who you really are by trusting your soul. Your friend "in" you will guide you to who you truly are. You are not really fear, you "are" love!

You will find it a little difficult to change immediately. You have been working from, and living with, fear for a great deal of time. Once you make the switch over to love, you will feel much happier. You will be the one who finds peace and you will know how to stay calm and carry on with your life regardless of circumstances.

This will create a new vibration within your body. Your body will begin to vibrate at a much higher rate and you will be affecting your own health. You will heal quickly and you will feel more positive than normal. This will be the turning point for you. You will want to tell everyone how content and happy you are. This is coming. This is you moving to your center and allowing peace of mind to settle in. You cannot allow peace to settle in you if, or when, you are busy wanting revenge. When you spend your thoughts, your power, your energy wanting others to be put down, you are literally putting you down. It cannot feel good to receive thoughts that say, "you're bad, you're not deserving, you should be punished and not receive good."

This is what you do to you when you find others guilty. Focus on the positive side of life and stop thinking about issues and situations that you cannot tolerate. Raise you up by lifting your thoughts to more positive and creative situations. Learn to send good healthy vibrations through you. Learn to send your power into your body in a positive, uplifting manner. "Use your power to create wisely!" Do not bring you down by focusing on bringing others down. I don't care if it's big business, or government, or politics or religious beliefs. Let it all go. If you cannot directly change or help a situation do not complain about it to your friends.

Now, do not go into black or white thinking here. Do not go to extremes. I am not telling you to accept abuse or destructive behavior. I am asking you to calm down until you can stand in a place of health and well being. Any abuse is not to be taken in. If you are physically threatened I suggest you run like hell. If you are verbally threatened leave; and if you are being emotionally abused run the other way. We have many traumatized people who are acting out and have moved into abnormal behavior. Leaving abuse is the best and most healthy way to handle it.

I am asking you, right now, to put down your verbal weapons. You talk big to impress your friends and you spout off about all that is wrong with the world, and this energy that you are spouting is affecting "you." You, the inner workings of you, go down in vibration every time you wish to put someone or something or some idea down. If you are reading a book titled *Journey into Your Soul,* you are more than likely looking for help and guidance. Do you wish to "lighten" your life and your thoughts and your feelings? Then this information is for you. Cause and effect is what we are learning in this class. If you do not care to learn about such things, that is your free will choice. You may go on to learn whatever you wish. If, however, you want to raise yourself and your attitude about life in general, I do believe I can assist you.

This is your opportunity to change and to move over to the light, the soul, the more tolerant part of you. Lift you up by lifting your thoughts up. It's really quite simple and will assist you in moving out of fear and into love. What you are full of is what you draw to you. If you see great chaos in your life you may wish to switch over to more peaceful thoughts. If you see struggle you may wish to calm yourself and flow with life. If you see pain, you might try self-love and self-nurturing and even self-praise. Psychological pain often leads to physical pain.

You may wish to check out a book that I wrote about in my original series of "Loving Light Books." It is titled *Heal Your Body* and was written by Louise Hay. This little book will give you great insight into the possible emotional cause of many physical ailments. I highly recommend this book to those of you who are in physical pain at this time.

When you move away from fear, you may frighten some of your family and friends. The programming and training on earth is very strongly supportive of protection at all costs. You even go so far as to accept killing in order to protect your own. You sanction killing in wartime "if" it is to defend your side and you allow for any type of defense that may be deemed possible. Bombs and missiles to protect have become common among nations. Now – there is no wrong way to live! Everything – absolutely everything is cause and effect. I am only trying to show you the areas in which you all agree that killing and death is okay.

Now; once you move away from fear, your friends may become concerned about your mental health. It is most common to live "in" fear and to convince our loved ones to fear what we fear. If we see danger we want everyone else to help fix the problem. Humans gather in groups for power and this allows them to feel safe. Most of your fears are around future "perceived" problems. There is not really a problem now but you see things as getting worse in the future and this causes most of your upset and stress and worry. "Live now!" Let go of any future "what ifs" and live in the now moment. Live for you, for your health and for your personal reality. Do not try to drag everyone else into your personal reality. Allow them to be who they are and they will allow you to be who you are. Do not be afraid to be God. Do not be afraid to be spirit. Do not be afraid to rise above the current level of fear energy.

❧❦

You will begin to notice little ways in which you judge life and situations. At those times you can change direction. It is as simple as catching a thought and replacing it with a positive, uplifting thought. Use ideas you may find hopeful or inspirational. Maybe you want a peaceful day, so you would turn your attention to peace and calm and harmony. Maybe you wish to let go of angry thoughts, so you would count to ten and tell yourself that everything will be okay and you will come through this situation on top. You may even use this positive thought technique when you are in pain. Simply tell yourself that you are "releasing" this problem from your body.

Often you will experience pain and emotions that are surfacing in order to heal you. You may have uprooted a past trauma or fear, or even a problem from a past life, or a parallel life, that is affecting you in the present moment. At these times, it will assist you if you look at what you are releasing or experiencing and ask yourself how it may possibly be a healing experience. It is most common for you to heal by retracing. By this I mean that you literally re-experience an old trauma, or pain, or sickness in order to release its energy from your body. Sometimes what you experience as a health problem is really the clearing of that problem from your cellular memory. All memory is energy and all energy moves. Usually energy moves in waves, and you may have layered past experiences in your cells, which are made up of billions and trillions of atoms. When you begin to raise your vibration, you literally dislodge old, dense energy from your body. You vibrate it loose and it crumbles from its solidified state and it begins to move, or float to the surface to be released. Most often you think you are getting sick or worse, when you are actually healing and getting better.

You are constantly changing and evolving with every thought and idea that you have. Thoughts are energy. You are an energy producing machine. You send out energy and you take in energy. You may change and you definitely may heal and get better. You may release old judgments that are holding you back and holding you down due to their weight. You may rise above your current state if you choose to do so. Everything is a choice. You may go left or you may go right. You may go up to a new level or you may stay where you are. You are never judged by God, you are only judged by you.

Once you learn to look upon illness as a possible clearing of old energy, you will give yourself the possibility of rising above the illness and coming out the other side. A positive outlook, or thought, when you do not feel well will assist your energy as it clears. Thoughts such as, "I am better and better every day," or, "I am strong and healthy," always assist you and move your vibration in an upward direction. You may also assure yourself that you will "experience the highest possible outcome." These thoughts, and staying calm, go a long way in assisting your body in times of illness. Do not be afraid, you are safe, you are loved and you are never-ending light.

So continue to express positive energy in order to raise you up, and continue to assist in the healing of you by expressing the positive and turning away from negative thought. You really don't want to move in that direction and you do want to be happy and healthy. You get what you put out, so I would suggest that you try happy and healthy thoughts about yourself, about your neighbors and about life in general. If you cannot see something in a positive light do not focus on it.

Now – here's the biggie: If you see war, begin to "believe" that everything will be okay in the end. Do not go "down" with what you are viewing. Your perception of the situation may not be a true version of events. Say a few souls volunteer to come to earth and act out violence and destruction and inhumanity, to assist those who are watching, in making positive choices regarding peace. What if someone or two someone's, planned to help a small child realize how his or her anger may lead to violence and harm? What if these two individuals put on a play for this child, to show him or her how anger is not healthy, and so they acted out violence and retribution on one another? This is, of course, only a demonstration, and these two actors are just pretending to hurt one another and in the end to die. This frightens the small child to the extent that he never again acts out his violence on another. He controls his angry thoughts and seeks peace at every turn.

Maybe, just maybe, certain souls volunteer to come in and show others how they do not really want war, which evolves from anger, which evolves from fear. Maybe they will be convinced by this demonstration to seek the more positive energy of love and acceptance. In life on earth, there are teachers and there are students. Your perspective may not include all information that is available, simply because you are operating from a lower level. When you rise up to a higher level, you will have a more expansive view and your perspective will rise above fear.

So, let it all be something that has meaning, until you can see the totality of life as a spirit that never ever dies. You are viewing life from the bottom of the mountain and to see the whole picture it would be a good idea to climb to the top.

It is well known on earth that you all make mistakes and none are perfect. Now is the time to realize that perfection is in the eye of the beholder. You do not require being perfect anymore than you require being God.

You already are perfection in that you have the ability to change and to grow into whatever choice you once made. You are a spirit who has entered matter in a desire to "create" from matter. When you are an energy being, you are only visible to those who exist in matter when you yourself are in matter. So all these spirit beings come here to the material world to play and have fun. You have fun with a body, which is basically the costume that you wear, and you have fun moving emotions up and down and you generally enjoy this experience in matter.

For the most part you have pretty much forgotten where you came from, how you got here and even why you came. You only know that you are human and you are having fun on the weekends and on holidays. This situation was all known to you before you entered a life on earth. You have been here before and you love to return. So I suggest you begin to enjoy your life just as it is and that you begin to accept that you may have come here to experience life as you now know it. Sometimes you choose a life path to learn something new that you didn't get the chance to experience in a previous life. Sometimes you return to learn how to remember, while in matter, who you really are; and sometimes you come here to bring in a little more awareness of what and who you truly are.

Sometimes spirits play this game where they wish to remember how they came into life and how they are really a light being inhabiting a body and not just a human walking around. Sometimes the game is to remember who you are and that you are only wearing a costume... this game may bring you out of your current game of victim/villain. This game may also bring you into the realm of higher consciousness. This game lifts you up and allows you to realize how you are a spirit, a soul, a being of light intelligence that is immersed in a dream. This being is actually having fun and enjoying this adventure.

Once you connect with and become aware of this part of yourself, you will begin to lighten up on your judgment of life and of people and of yourself. You will begin to appreciate the fact that you chose to come here and that this is just a game. You will begin to wake up to the fact that you are a soul, a being of light who is all knowing and all loving and certainly all accepting of everything that you see. Why are you so all accepting of all that you see? Simply because you are aware that this is not real. It is make believe. It is fun and games. It is a movie and you are acting a part. You may get creative and act this part in any way that you wish. You may find villains at every turn, or you might want to find heroes and love and kindness and generosity at every turn.

It is all there for your pleasure. You may look at whatever interests you. If you find places of peace, you are searching for peace. If you find love and kindness, you are searching for love and kindness. You will focus on that which is strongest "in" you. If you let go of judgment, you will begin to see acceptance. If you let go of fear you will begin to see love. And if you let go of your own guilt, you will begin to see innocence. You only see what is "in" you because what is "in" you draws more of the same to you. If you wish to see less negativity in the world stop looking at it and focusing on it. Begin to see it differently by looking for something good. If you see war, then focus on all those who are helping and giving aid. Do not focus on what you judge as bad and begin to look for the good in absolutely everything.

Now; when you begin to see good in everything, do not shout at those who are still focusing on the bad. They will not wish to hear your report of good behavior and they will, more than likely, try to convince you to join their fear of how awful life can be. If you wish to rise above duality, it is helpful to keep your new perspective to yourself until you are standing firmly in a place of positivity. This will allow you to accept yourself in this new position before you begin your ascent into the higher realms of thinking. You are rising above the forces of chaos and negativity. Energy flows in waves and you don't want to get knocked off your pedestal of higher truth on your first rise up.

So, keep your perspective close to your heart as you begin to join forces with the spirit/soul "in" you who knows that this is just a fun game that souls play. You are a soul who has come to earth to play and to wake up and remember who you really are while still in matter. No more waiting for death to remember that you only pretend to die and you are actually a never-ending being of light. Why not join forces with this part of yourself now? Why not begin to see life differently right now? Why not begin to see you differently right now?

⁂

Now is a good time to remind you that you are human as well as spirit. You are not expected to have all the answers or to be perfect in your behavior. Perfection is always in the eye of the beholder, and in the eyes of spirit, you are perfect just the way you are. It is all a game and it is supposed to be fun.

So; as you begin your day, I wish you to remember that you have an energy light being right inside of you who loves and accepts you just the way you are. There is no need to change anything unless you desire to do so. You need not wake up to the fact that you contain light in every cell of your body, and there is no need for you to acknowledge that you are God in human form. Everything is simply a choice and is an option. Every option creates its own unique effect and each effect may lead you to yet another option. You are not bad. You are not sinners and you do no wrong. You have not displeased God. You never could displease God and you are made of God energy. You have only been taught and trained that you are lost and must save your soul from hell fire and damnation. Do not believe it and do not buy into it if you choose not to. It is always your free will to buy what others are selling, and often the ones who are encouraging you to save your soul are very fearful in their own beliefs.

When people are full of fear, they want to warn you of the dangers they see ahead. Usually, preconceived danger is a manifestation of fear. When held in place, fear will grow and draw more fear to it. This is how cults are formed. They have a leader, or leaders, who spread the fear and it sucks in vulnerable adults and children. The fear, once set in place in the cells of the body, will then attract more fear due to the magnetic nature of energy.

So; let go of fear and you will begin to drain it from your cells and your body. Do not allow others to pull you down in this way. God does not punish you. God has never punished you, and it is safe to "believe" that God, who resides within you, is all loving and all accepting and never ever judges you. Man got it a little confused when he changed God from nonviolent and loving to violent and punishing.

When you fear God, you are fearing you. God is in you. You come from God and are made from the stuff of God. You are God light in a physical form. There is nothing wrong or bad about you or about anything you have ever done. This is all an illusion, a dream. Please let go of the idea that you could displease God in any way. I am not a judge – that is man's fear talking. I do not harm you – ever! You are me, I am you!

Please let go of your fear of a punishing God and it will assist you in letting go of the guilt that you carry about so many things. God does not punish and God does not keep score of your mistakes and what you, and others, consider bad behavior. There is no bad behavior. There is nothing you can do to displease God. You are innocent. You are pure just as you are. You are free to be you, no rules, no commandments and no punishment. Live your life "freely"– free from guilt, free from punishment and free from emotional trauma. Let God in your life, not the God of religion and rules and commandments, but the God of love and acceptance. Allow yourself the freedom of letting go of all the training and programming from earth perspectives. To come here to earth you must go unconscious because of the density of this playground. To come to this playground you must let go of your self-awareness and pretend to be dumb to who you truly are.

You have gone unconscious and you made it into your little realm of matter. Now the fun begins as you wake up to who you truly are by remembering your connection to God, to All That Is, to the Light of all. You are the light pretending that you are not light. And what is the opposite of light? It is darkness... you have pretended to be something that you are not in order to enter the playground. It is time now... it is okay now if you wish to return to your true identity.

❧

For the most part you are afraid. You are afraid of hatred and you are afraid of love. You fear that those who hate you will bring harm to you in some way and you are afraid that those who love you will hurt you in some way.

So, the best thing for you to do is to let go of expectations. Do not insist that those you care about behave in a specific manner. Live and let live. Allow everyone to be who they are and you be you. Focus on your behavior and let go of focusing on everyone else. Do you see people as stupid and ignorant? This is now you judging you as stupid and ignorant. You wonder why you have low self-esteem and low self-worth. I will tell you now that you were trained in childhood how to treat yourself. If your parent or guardian said, "No, you are doing it wrong," you may have thought "I am so stupid and I do everything wrong." When you entered school as a small child and you were again told, "No, you are doing it wrong," you may have thought, "How dumb am I, I will never learn to be smart." Then, as you moved on to higher grades, you heard more of "You are doing it wrong."

Once you graduated (or not) you probably moved into the job force and were again told how you do not do the job correctly. This, of course, is during your training period at your new job. As you learn your job and how to do it correctly, you may or may not be praised and awarded big raises. This may lead to the underlying assumption that you do not know how to do it right. Often this type of training leaves you insecure in your position and fearful of losing your job.

Most of your training has been to teach you how to survive and, in some cases, to thrive in this three dimensional world. However, you have already developed low self-worth and you begin to resent it every time someone tells you that the way you see life is not the correct way. You now begin to fear retribution from those who do not like what you like and you find it difficult to accept those who are too different from you. You feel safer when you are around those you can relate to and you feel, or may feel, uncomfortable around those you cannot relate to.

This is fear. You all contain fear and you all operate from fear. It is good to know this and to begin to let go of fear. Fear does not kill you, but it does take you down energy wise. Fear is dense and heavy and exhausting. Fear is considered the opposite of love because hatred comes from fear. When you hate someone, or something, it is because you fear them or it.

Now; as you go along in your healing process, you will begin to let go of fear and this will allow you to move over to love. Love will set you free. Love is not hugging your enemy and sitting down to dinner with him or her. Love is the energy equivalent to acceptance. It's like knowing that you have a neighbor and allowing them to be part of the neighborhood. You need not socialize if you do not feel moved to do so. You simply allow them their space and you allow you your space.

Once you learn acceptance, you will automatically be letting go of the energy of judgment that has been weighing you down and magnetically drawing greater judgment to you. You will begin to realize how you have been "trained" to judge and to discern and to make good choices, and this has gone too far to one side. Discernment has turned to "I deserve to be treated better than those who do not deserve." You have gone too far in your protection of self and now, because you are so full of fear, you believe that everyone is out to get you, or that you will not get your fair share. This, of course, is due to the fact that you believe that others, who you see as beneath you, do not deserve a break; and this in turn is due to the basic fact that you carry low self-worth and so you are judging others as not worthy. These others may be the poor who do not work and achieve as you think they should, or these others may be those who are wealthy and have achieved a great deal. You are afraid that you will not get your fair share and so you blame others for their behavior and sometimes you resent their way of life.

Just let it go! It is all a reflection of what is inside of you. You can only see what is in you. You cannot see what is in another. Their lives and their past lives are part of their programming. You will not heal you by trying to fix everyone else. Let it go! Heal you! Focus on you! Love you and nurture you! Take good care of you and you will begin to come into balance.

Once you come into balance you will see others differently simply because your reflection will change. You will no longer be sending out revenge and resentment and so you will no longer "feel" revenge and resentment. This means that all those you hate, or can't stand, will fade away. Your hatred of self is strong depending on how much you dislike yourself for not having all the right moves and correct answers. You will no longer hate anyone once you love you. Love begins at home in you, not out there in your mirror. Your mirror is only reflecting what you are, not what they are.

Let go of hatred by letting go of your fear. After all "love is letting go of fear" as Mr. Jampolsky wrote. Now; I want to highly recommend this little book to you. I first made it available to Liane many years ago and it served her well. I highly recommend it and the title is of course, *Love is Letting Go of Fear*. It is by a wonderful healer, Mr. Jerry (Gerald) Jampolsky. This book will guide you as you learn to let go of your fear.

꧁꧂

*F*or the longest time you have felt alone. You feel like you are alone and misunderstood in your ideas and your feelings about life in general. It is not often that you find someone who really gets you and totally sees how you see life. This is due to the fact that you are all layered differently. You have experienced your own unique situations in life and you have drawn your own unique perspectives based on those experiences. Now, add to that all experiences from past lives and you have quite a list of events and learning lessons.

Because you have all your own experiences, you are convinced that your way and your fears and even your upsets are justified. They may be simply an effect of a specific cause. Say you were traumatized as a small child by seeing some violent act on television or in a movie; now, whenever you even hear about anyone who shows violence, you have a very strong reaction and you judge this person as a bad person. This is how judgment works. You see something as harmful and it leaves an imprint on your nervous system. Now, in your current life, this same situation might occur and it is not at all harmful to you; however you still carry that imprint from childhood or even past life.

Every event in your life today is being weighed and measured against every situation you have ever seen and allowed to affect you emotionally. As you go through life you weigh everyone and everything against what occurred in the past, or even on television. Please watch positive situations in your movies and on TV until you can bring your nervous system into balance. You spend a great deal of time moving to the fear side of you because of the fearful negativity that you are taking in. It will help a great deal if you stop feeding yourself drama and traumatic excitement. Your nervous system does not know that the person being shot in your movie is just an actor and is not dying, in the same way that your nervous system does not know that the person on your news who was shot is not dying and is an everlasting soul being.

Please be kind to your nervous system until you can clear and release some of these harsh judgments that you carry. You know you have harsh judgments and fear in you by the amount of resentment and revenge that you carry. If you just can't stand someone, or some idea, look closely at your fear. If you come into balance, you will no longer feel angry about politics and about specific belief systems that are different than yours. You are only holding a different belief system because you are layered differently and, therefore, programmed differently. Their fears are still fear, as are your fears. You have just taken a different road because you were programmed and trained differently. You are all the same in that it is all a matter of fear and of how much fear.

Do you act out on friends and family or on enemies and strangers? Are you feeling like you don't fit in? It may be that you are judging everyone including life, or it may be that you have so much blame and guilt built up "in" you that you are now judging "you" harshly. Remember – all that judgment against others ends up sitting inside of you, not them.

"Judge not lest ye be judged" is an exactitude. You are harming you and causing you to struggle through life. You may let go of your struggle with life by going with the flow. Once you stop adding more judgment to you, you will begin to feel better and it will become easier for you to get along with life just as it is. This is what you all want. You all want to get along and when you do get along, you will find peace.

Peace comes when struggle ends. Peace comes when you put down your weapons of disagreement and unrest. Peace comes when you no longer find one way the right way. Peace comes when duality is overcome. Duality is overcome when you let go of right and wrong and move into understanding how everyone is operating from fear and lack of understanding. Peace can begin with you. Lay down your verbal weapons and begin to listen and understand. This will open the door to peace in your personal life and you will begin to flow with your life.

You want war to end? You may be the first in your neighborhood to learn the secret: "Peace begins right inside of you." And because you are a vibrating energy being who emits what is in you, guess what you will be sending out into the world and into your personal reality? You are really love and you have only moved into fear temporarily. You will come home to love, it is what you are.

꧁꧂

You are wonderful! You are the most beautiful creation and you are from God. You have the creative force of the Source of "all that is" right inside of you. You have this most wonderful being existing "in" you and you barely recognize its existence. Now is a good time to begin to see you differently. See yourself as a soul who is walking this planet and enjoying this excursion into the material realm. Let go of your belief that you are a human who is dumb and awkward, and begin to see the beauty in yourself. See you as a spirit who is simply playing and enjoying life on earth. Let go of all seriousness and you will begin to lighten up a bit. This is not a time to focus on what is wrong with you, this is a time to focus on how you would look if you truly saw the light being that you are.

If you could see the beautiful soul that you truly are, you would be in awe. You would fall to your knees in gratitude and you would change how you perceive life in general. You would know how you are much greater than you ever dreamed and you would no longer fear anything about life or about death. If you could be your soul for just one day, you would "trust" that anything and everything that happens here is okay. You would let go of worry and you would become so much lighter and even healthier. In the letting go of fear and worry, you would be allowing fear and worry to leave your cells. Once fear has drained from your body, there will no longer be the down pull on the energy that is you. You would no longer struggle to rise above the denseness that has been holding you down.

When you move over to love and trust and acceptance, you will rise quickly to the lighter energies that make up love, trust and acceptance. The more you fear the idea of trust and acceptance, the greater your need for them.

So, what do you say? Can you be the first on your block to move into love? Or will you continue to live in fear? It is all up to you and, as I often have told you, there is no wrong way and no right way. Your soul loves and accepts all choices and will never be disappointed in you. Your soul is simply waiting patiently for the opportunity to drive. Your soul would love to guide you into new adventures and to new heights. This is possible and may be accomplished upon request. No one may override your free will and so everything is done according to your wishes. You are a free will energy source and you will continue to live and to create according to your own wishes. You may go as high as you wish or you may stay as low as you like. There is no wrong choice. It is no different than standing on a mountaintop or standing in a valley. Each gives you a place to stand and each gives you an adventure here on earth.

So, bottom line is, you are beautiful if you choose to rise above to a new perspective and you are also beautiful if you choose to stay where you are. I think you might enjoy the lightness of being that comes from a higher perspective and you could use the break from fear; however, you may be comfortable (now) and feel afraid of rising higher. It is your free will choice and I only guide and suggest, I do not push you.

Now is a good time to remind you that you are a soul, a spirit being, as well as a human, and you are capable of great feats of strength. You create and you move into your creations. You are where you are now because you have created this life for yourself without knowing that you did. You are already God and you are already creating on certain levels. It might be fun to consciously create and to be "aware" that you are a soul who is inside of a body and is guiding from that position. Why not make friends with your soul? Why not get in touch with that part of yourself? Why not continue your life with a friend who not only gets you, but totally loves and accepts you? Wouldn't it be fun to have someone you can lean on and who only wants the best for you? Wouldn't it be fun to have your own personal guide in life, and wouldn't it be fun to know that you are never ever alone?

You have a great deal to learn about who you truly are and how you create. You are just now beginning your inner journey, your journey into your soul self.

⁂

*Y*ou have always been a creative light being, however, you have not always been human. You come into this material world to play. It is like living in a house then going outside the house to play. You don't really go outside of God, but you get the idea.

As you continue to journey outside to play, you always leave part of you behind. You have many areas of you and you actually take up all time and all space. There really is nothing but you and you are everlasting, never-ending, always moving and changing energy. Part of you is "in" you and part of you is in your neighbor and in his neighbor. You are all that is and you come from Source and you are Source. It is like the analogy of a drop from the ocean containing all aspects and properties of the ocean. You are vast indeed and you have the ability to focus on a tiny area and then create an entire make believe world from that area. You may create many different illusions while existing in many different bodies.

You are the yin and the yang of all life. You exist everywhere all at once. If you could see all of you, you would be in awe of your greatness and of your creative abilities. You have the power and the ability to shape shift and to become anything you can possibly imagine. You simply see it and you become it. However, you are still you! You are still your Source. You are always connected to all of you. Energy does not have boundaries and when you are "All That Is," you are everything and everywhere. You are part of everything because your Source energy flows through and into everything. Energy has no boundaries. Energy moves through and in and around absolutely everything. You cannot stop the flow and movement of energy as it is not possible.

In the same way that you cannot stop the movement of a stream of water, you cannot stop the movement of energy. You may build dams and walls but the water is still moving and shifting and changing. This is what you are... you are energy in motion. You leave the majority of you out of each individual human body, as you are vast indeed. You only send a tiny portion of your energy into each human form that you inhabit. You then focus on that particular form and call it you. Which form do you call you? It is the one you happen to be focusing on right now. You have the creative ability to bring your focus, or attention, down to a tiny pinpoint of light and inject it into a form and, by doing so, wear that form and call it your own.

Then you repeat this process again and again and again for as many times and as many different creations as you would like to express. So now we have you the dog, and you the tree, and you the rock, and you the earth, and you who is reading this, and you your neighbor, and you the ruler in another country, and you the slave, and you the ax murderer, and you the saint, and it is all you. You are the one and only Source expressing through and playing in matter. Get over it! Allow everyone to be and get over fighting with all other you's. Know you and love you as you are in your many forms. You are God expressing through matter and it is no big deal. It is what God does. It is energy in movement and it is creation constantly being created. Get over it and let it be. Accept God as is. Let God be. Let yourself be acceptable and let all of life on earth be acceptable, until you can figure out who you truly are and who you truly want to be. You are part of a giant, never-ending, creative force and you have gone unconscious to the fact that you are. Because you are unconscious you have been judging life. Get over it! Let it go! Stop being so negative! Stop finding everything you do not like and begin to accept life on earth.

This is all for today. I would like you to walk into your life today and appreciate the beauty of all that you are and all that life is....

෨ฬ෮

𝓕or the first time you will unite two very big parts of you... the human mind and spirit. The human mind has been programmed to believe everything that it believes and everything that it fears. The spirit/soul knows without reasoning… it simply knows. It is aware and has understanding that is beyond human understanding. The human mind can understand only after evaluating and proving to itself.

The way to rise above human understanding is to trust spiritual knowledge. Spirit is by far more aware and awake and in the know. If you can learn to allow spirit to guide you, you will no longer need judgment. With soul awareness you will find less struggle and greater peace. You will not have the need to question whether you are moving in the right direction or not. You will simply "know" where and what will bring you the higher vibrations of love, peace and joy. Life will no longer be a struggle and you will feel much lighter and much happier.

This, of course, is not the normally accepted way to operate on earth and will require some getting accustomed to. You will find yourself learning as you go and it will be a matter of switching from mental leadership to soul leadership. This involves your intuition. Most times your soul is guiding you via your intuition. Sometimes you may end up in a situation you did not expect and many times this situation will lead to new avenues of friendship or even prosperity. You will find these new areas increasing your level of happiness and making life easier. Your soul, via intuition, is always trying to help you as you navigate life on earth. This does not mean that your soul will simply tell you all your answers or even show you. Your soul will, however, guide you in the direction that will best serve you. If you land in a situation that you do not like, it may be that it is serving a higher purpose and you should pay attention and look for the gift in this particular situation.

When you require healing, you may be guided to a particular doctor who will find your disease or you may be guided to information that will give you guidance in self-healing.

Both ways serve you and both ways are valid choices. Once you find where you belong, you will begin to heal and to come into balance.

You are sometimes afraid of healing simply because it means you must change in some way. Usually it means you must take better care of your physical body. Sometimes it is a matter of taking better care of your mental body and your emotional body. In all cases it is a matter of loving yourself enough to want to take real good care of you. Often you are taught to care for and nurture others but not necessarily yourself. You are taught from childhood to love and respect your siblings and your family members. But rarely are you taught to love and nurture yourself. Life is too busy for many parents and they find it stressful emotionally. When the parents are stressed the children, who have always been told "no, you are doing it wrong," begin to blame themselves. When a child is in its training and developmental phase, he/she will often believe that when things go wrong it is always his/her fault. This, of course, leads to low self-worth and grows sometimes into self-hatred.

When a child is harshly punished, or manipulated, in order to cover wrongdoing by the parent, the child will grow up blaming itself for anything that goes wrong within the family. This is due to misunderstanding and misperception and confused thinking. It is often a product of childhood and it is one that may require healing in adulthood. So now we have all these self-blaming children who hate themselves for all the mistakes they "believe" they have caused and they are the walking wounded. Sometimes the wounds you carry in your adult life are emotional and mental wounds caused by your own misinterpretation of childhood events. Sometimes the wounds you carry affect your adult life and your thinking and reasoning process. Sometimes the wounds that you carry cause you to become very, very defensive, and the idea of someone telling you, "no, you are wrong in your thinking," will set you off. Your wounds are still in you and you suffer if they are driving your life. Allow spirit to drive for a while. Let go of your defensiveness and turn everything over to God – not the God of religion, but the God "in" you.

"Let go and let God" is a very good axiom. Use it often. Talk to your mind. Talk to yourself. Allow yourself to know that you are ready to love and nurture you. Allow yourself to know that you did nothing wrong! Allow yourself to know that it was all a big mistake, a big misunderstanding. Allow yourself to know that you are safe and you will never ever be punished for your sins in childhood. Let yourself know that you are loved just the way you are with no need or requirement for you to behave a certain way.

This life on earth is meant to be fun and games. Let go of all your programming and begin to create life how you want it to be. Do you want to lighten up and not take it all so seriously? Then that is what you will get. You get what you focus on the most. The energy moves in that direction and that part of your life begins to grow. Do not tell your friends that you are no longer going to focus on war and suffering. They will not think that is a good idea. Keep your new found insight, on how to create a peaceful happy life, to yourself until you are strong in your peace and happiness. You were never meant to take on the problems of this three dimensional world, you were meant to rise above them.

*Y*ou have been on a roller coaster of ups and downs since you can remember. This is due to the fact that you take on new fears, which bring you down, and then you level out. Once you have leveled out at this new lower level, you begin to adjust and to be okay with it. Then, after some time, you have taken on enough new fear that you go down one more level, and after some time you level out once again.

As you age, you tend to take on more and more fear. This fear allows you to go further down energy wise. As your energy slows its vibration, you begin to adjust to each new level. You basically drop yourself into an energy vortex or hole. You go down, down, down when you could be going up, up, up. Once you change direction by letting go of your hold on fear, you will begin to raise your vibration to the next level. Then, as you let go of more judgment based fear, you will move "up" once again and level off to balance yourself. This will continue as you rise up in this ascension process. You are basically going up in the same way that you went down.

As you rise, you may begin to "feel" the denser energy of fear that you are releasing. This could be any fear energy from anger to sorrow or from revenge to resentment. You may find yourself getting angry or sad for no reason. This may be due to a release of energy simply from taking on the energy of acceptance. Acceptance allows judgment to cease, which in turn allows all the energy that judgment has created, to rise to the surface and leave your body. It will be as though your cells and atoms are sloughing off the energy that has been trapped in them for so long. When you feel these emotions rise to the surface, allow them to flow through you and do not act on them. Allow your emotional body to heal and to release these energy charges that have been created by fear.

Allow yourself to rest and to be calm. Create a peaceful, loving environment around yourself and avoid outside drama if possible. Remember – you are magnetic in nature and you draw to you what you contain in the way of energy. So, if you are healing and, in so doing, emitting or sloughing off some form of anger or sorrow, you may draw some form of angry or sad event to you. Always stay in communication with your inner self so you may know what you are healing and/or releasing in the way of energy. Always remember to count to ten (maybe make it one hundred) if you find yourself being triggered at these vulnerable times.

Life is always moving and changing and you are always moving and changing. Learn to accept your emotions and guide them in a healthy and happy direction. Tell yourself that this will pass which it will, and stay calm until any storm, emotional or otherwise, subsides. You are dealing with energy and thoughts and feelings. You are an energy being. You are okay just as you are. You are healing, and each time you release a little dense energy, you rise up to the next energy level. It is like climbing a ladder and sometimes you need to stop and catch your breath. Do not judge you for being human with emotions. You have always feared your emotional body and now is a time of acceptance of all of you. No part of you will be left out as you begin to heal body, mind and spirit. It is all coming into balance. All is well. Stay calm and be at peace. You are simply learning and opening up to, and beginning to accept... and therefore love you.

❧

You have always been a species of worry and anger, it is programmed into you. So now you want to be joyful and happy and worry free. The way to be worry free is to let go of your fear.

Fear is basically an emotion that is connected to your thoughts. It is directly a result of being concerned that an event will or will not occur. Say you want a raise in pay but you do not think you will receive your raise before the rent is due. This creates a problem for you because you have no savings and you are worried about where you will live if, or when, you might be evicted. Do not set this idea up in your mind! Instead set up the idea that you will receive the best possible outcome for yourself. Know (in your mind) that something will happen to change your circumstance for the better. All energy that is sent out from you will come back to you in some form. You also live in the energy that is in you and around you. Give yourself a chance to see a better life and you will draw better energy to you.

If you came into this dimension with the purpose of being poor, you may not wish to rise above poverty. You may wish to continue playing the poor role and this too is okay. If, however, you wish to grow in a new direction and create a different outcome for yourself, you may do so. The energy you draw to yourself is directly connected to what you carry within you. You may change from a scarce and limited view and allow yourself greater abundance. Do not blame yourself and do not condemn yourself to a life you do not want. Begin to see the good in life and you will draw more good to you. I realize there is no good or bad in reality, but you decide something is good and that makes it desirable.

If you find that you have great resentment towards the wealthy and those in power positions due to wealth, you may be blocking your own wealth. After all, you cannot draw something to you if you do not embrace it. If you constantly focus on poverty, you will more than likely block wealth.

Poverty is a way of living and is acceptable. If you are constantly focusing on being without, you are sending a great deal of energy "into" being without and you are making it grow bigger. Remember – you make your enemies bigger by giving them power. Do not feed or water a plant if you do not want it to grow.

Now, I would be remiss if I did not mention more information regarding financial wealth. I have written a book titled, *For the Love of Money,* and this book may be helpful to you and explain in greater detail how gratitude may assist you. For now I will leave you with this thought: You live in a world that is made up and not real. This world is affected by the energy you want or don't want in your life. Always focus on what you want and do not put any energy into a scenario that you do not wish to draw to you.

~ ❧ ~

*F*or the most part you believe that you will never be reconnected with true unconditional love. You believe that it is impossible to know everything and be aware of everything and even to accept everything.

You will learn that you are very immature in your development. You are at a phase in your evolution into matter that is quite dense and difficult to see through. From where you are it is difficult to see God, or your Source. It is difficult to feel your true nature of unconditional love and acceptance because you are blocked from doing so. It is like trying to see and feel the sun on a very cloudy day. The trick is to get those clouds out of the way so that you might feel and enjoy the gifts that come from God, your Source.

So, we have a plan, from now on you will allow any cloud "in" you to leave. You will allow any hurt feeling or emotional wound to leave. You will do this by letting go of your need to hold a grudge. You will let go of all those harsh judgments you hold against thoughts, ideas and actions that you personally can't stand the thought of. You will clear some of your clutter and cloudiness by allowing for the possibility that maybe; just maybe, there is a reason for everything.

I want you to begin to wonder why others believe as they do. You will begin to see that it is mostly due to genetics and also it is due to environment. You will also find that rules and traditions have a big effect on others. Once you begin to realize how others are trained and programmed to see life differently than you, it will be easier for you to understand how you are also programmed and trained and sometimes coerced to see life as you now see it. This will allow you to understand diversity of thoughts and beliefs. You will find that most people simply believe what they believe as a response to how they are perceiving life.

If you constantly see life and others, who are different in their behavior, as dangerous, you will wish to come to your center and become more balanced in your perception. You are simply over protecting yourself and this can easily lead to paranoia in certain situations. Do not jump to "danger" in your mind every time the least little thing goes wrong. Right now what you need is trust. Trust God, your Source, and trust life. You did not come here to bring in fear; you came here in an attempt to enjoy this journey and maybe to wake up to your true identity while still in matter. You may do this. This is very doable.

Look; if you were meant to come to earth and hide from life on earth, there wouldn't be much point in it. If you were unmolested and un-traumatized in childhood, you probably

84

enjoyed your childhood and played without a care in the world. Fear is programmed into you. You may have fear from past lives and you may have fear from this life. All fear is energy that tells you to not trust. The greater your fear the less trust you will have. So, the first step is to get you to realize that your fear not only holds you back, your fear also holds you down on the ground. It is impossible to fly when you are weighted down.

When you take in fear, you literally add weight and density to you. You become heavy and rigid and very judgmental. It's time now to release some fear. It's time now to let it go. I want you to go into your fears until they dissolve away. Fear is usually based on a preconceived idea about someone or something. Fear is usually based on a future probability, e.g., "What if this happens or what if that happens?" Let go of these preconceived ideas and replace them with, "I will experience the best possible outcome." Let go of programming yourself for greater fear and begin to program yourself for love.

Affirmations are a good place to start. In the same way that your parents may have programmed and trained you by constantly repeating what they wanted you to learn, you may constantly repeat your affirmations to reprogram yourself to accept love of yourself. Self-love affirmations are the best. Why? Simply because love is the answer to everything and when you are in a state of self-love you are drawing more love to you. When in a state of fear, you draw more fear to you. So, self-love is the ticket out of fear. You may choose to use recorded messages to help you get started with your self-love training.

When you begin to love you and accept you, it will make it easier for you to love and accept others. You are at a turning point and the road ahead is bright and filled with light and weightlessness. You are headed in a very joyful and happy direction. You have been fear and now you are changing and you are becoming love. You are what you feed yourself. Feed you less fear of "what ifs" and more trust that "all will be well." This will bring you a wonderful feeling of well-being and with well-being "in" you, you will always do well!

⚡

*W*hen you begin to wake up, you will be amazed at how good you will feel. The feeling of well-being is a very peaceful state of being. You will learn to flow with life in a way that makes your days enjoyable. As you flow, you will begin to accept all the little things that you now judge. When things go wrong for you, you tend to get upset and this only compounds the situation. The ideal response when things go wrong is to be aware that this is happening for a reason and you are not aware of that reason.

Say your car won't start in the morning and you need to get to work. Maybe, just maybe, if your car would have started in time you would have been sitting at that stoplight when the truck came barreling through, crashing into everyone because its breaks went out. Always trust the flow of your life and you will begin to flow more easily with all situations that come to you. Remember – you are magnetic in nature and you draw to you what you are. If you carry a great deal of revenge you may draw greater revenge to you. Your soul may choose to assist you when you have put yourself in a difficult situation. Sometimes, when you have a close call, you might lift your eyes up to heaven and say, "Thank you God," and this is your soul at work assisting you.

When you draw uncomfortable situations, it is often to show yourself how you can solve situations and rise above the chaos. You do not trust life and this translates to, you do not trust "you." You run the energy of mistrust through your body day and night. Some of you even have trouble sleeping because you are constantly on guard, waiting for, or preparing for, the next thing to go wrong. It is time now to come over to trust. I know this is difficult for you and you have spent all these years trying to protect yourself and keep you safe, but it is time to trust. I want you to trust yourself by trusting your soul. I want you to run the energy of trust through your body so that you might release some of that mistrust and fear and tension that you carry in your cells.

Give your body a break. Give your mind a break! You may live your life differently than you have been trained. Begin to focus on the good in life and in you. You are good... you are loved... you are safe. Surrender now! Turn your life over to your higher self, your soul self, the part of you who will guide you back to your Source. You spend all your time imagining the dreams you want and then you put out all this energy that says, "You are not good enough, I do not like you," simply because you do not like the others who live on this planet or you think they do not deserve.

You are canceling out your own dreams and desires by running all this conflicting energy through you, your body. So now I would like you to let it all go! Do not envision what you think will make you happy, simply envision being happy. Do not envision the big job that will bring you the prosperity you want, simply envision being prosperous and happy. And do not envision that perfect mate who will love you, simply envision you loving you. You may move quicker to self-love by loving and accepting you just as you are. You will then begin to love everyone, and you will realize how you are all the same and let go of your fear of them.

You are really fearing you, as you do not really trust you. You have been trained and programmed to believe that you are not trustworthy. Your "perception" and your take away from all those times you were told, "no, you are not doing it right" got to you and now you are in a big hole of mistrust. Come up out of your hole. Come to the light of acceptance. You did nothing wrong and you could never ever do anything wrong in the eyes of God. God, your source, does not judge you ever! This is not real! You are love and light and you are part of God. Love you! Trust you! Let go and surrender to the love of God that resides right inside of you. Open to love, to God, to soul.

☙✲❧

𝒥or the first time since you came to earth, you are about to understand why you came. It is not easy to be unconscious and driving in the dark. You will learn to depend on your soul, or spirit, to move you and to assist in your little adventure.

Once you become aware that you have this part of you who is always observing and watching over you, you will feel loved and looked out for. You will no longer feel so alone and so forgotten. You will feel like you are embraced by a part of you that not only loves you, but also is you. You will begin to move over to self-love and this will feel so very good after a lifetime of feeling alone in your ideas and your life.

Once you become comfortable communicating with this part of you, you will begin to feel a little safer and even nurtured by spirit energy. You all have this part of you and this part of you is patiently waiting to be accepted and acknowledged. This part of you "is" love and is the energy of love. This part of you is aware that you are part of God/All That Is/Source, and it is patiently waiting for you to become aware of this fact.

This part of you is able to inspire you to great ideas and great movement forward. This soul in you is who you truly are and is always with you. This soul in you is waiting and will always accept you "just as you are." You need not wait until someday when you are better or more loving or less afraid. This higher part of you wishes only to assist you in your journey and life on earth. This higher part of you vibrates and exists inside of every atom and molecule that makes you up. You might say that the core of you is God, or Source. You might say that the basic makeup of you is your soul. You are soul energy in a body.

So, here is the big gift – you may begin to communicate with your own soul now! You may talk to your soul and ask for guidance in your life now. You may wish to communicate and befriend your soul now. It may be as simple as saying "good morning" when you wake up or "good night" when you lay down to sleep. Begin to know that you are soul energy by acknowledging the existence of your own soul energy. As you continue to communicate with your soul, you will find that your awareness of soul energy will increase. Remember – what you focus on will grow. Focus on the love part of you. Focus on the higher part of you. Focus on your own God self and you will grow in that direction.

≈‖≈

*Y*ou have always wanted to be happy and so you constantly focus on things that you think will bring you happiness. Why not focus on happiness? Let go of your need to have things and people in your life who you think will bring you joy and begin to focus on joy.

You tend to wish for and want things and once you acquire them you are happy for a moment and then you are no longer happy. When you focus on the acquiring of things, then you are happy with the acquiring and that begins to fade fairly quickly. You are happy with the idea of getting your desires and the getting, or receiving, is short lived. As you focus on the end result you will be allowed to live in the end result. If you think a trip abroad will make you happy then you will be, or may be, happy during your trip. When your trip ends, your happy feelings may fade with your memory of your trip. Always focus on what you really want, and what you really want is not usually a one time event. What you really want is joy and peace and love.

So how do we focus on joy, peace and love? We begin to feel joy and we begin to feel peace and we begin to feel love. Feel a memory – any memory that brought you joy. Then hold that memory for a moment. Then bring that memory feeling up again and re-experience it again and again. Do this with peace and with love. You have had at least one peaceful moment in your life, and you can catch that memory and hold it in your mind until you feel it once again. Then do this on a daily basis... bring peace to the surface and feel it for moments, then for hours, then for days.

You can be the one to bring peace to your own life and this will enable you to send peaceful energy out into your personal world and your earth world. You are an energy being who creates and emits energy. Begin to send out positive energy and you will eventually find yourself living in a world of positivity and peace.

Do not be afraid to be positive in your thoughts. I know the world teaches you to not be happy if anyone is suffering, however, as mentioned before – you do not know what the true reality of this game on earth is. You do not know because you are unconscious and cannot see what is really being created. Stay calm and breathe and emit "peace" and you will begin to see how peace is actually being created in a way that you do not understand.

When you begin to create your own peace, it will begin to grow. Why? Simply because you will be tuning in to peace. You are God, the creator of all that is, and you receive what you focus on; and the greater your focus the bigger the situation gets. So; you may save the world by saving you. Go positive! Think positive! Do not concern yourself with what everyone else is doing. Be you... be God... create peace by feeling peace and you will be letting go of fear and anger and dense energy inside of you. Heal you through peace and joy. Bring your energy up to peace and joy, and then you will find your precious self-love. Love you by changing your energy. Change your channel to love. Watch a new life movie and you will begin to tune in to all the peace and joy and happiness that is all around you. You simply do not see it because you are too busy focusing on everything that is wrong. Change your mind please!

―――――――――― ❢ ――――――――――

By using brain imaging, Dr. Richard J. Davidson, a neuroscientist, and others have found that positive emotions can trigger "reward" pathways located deep within the brain, including in an area known as the ventral striatum.

"Individuals who are able to savor positive emotions have lasting activation in the ventral striatum," Davidson says. "The longer the activation lasts, the greater his or her feelings of well-being." Continued activation of this part of the brain has been linked to healthful changes in the body, including lower levels of a stress hormone.

–National Institute of health

You will find that the closer you get to waking up, the better you will feel. Your worries and concerns will drop away and you will begin to trust the process of life. The more you focus on how good life is, the more good, or desirable, you will receive from life.

Always look for the good in everything and always look for the good in you. You are a multi-dimensional being of light... how amazing is that? You are part of God awareness that is operating inside a human. You are beyond human comprehension and yet you exist within a human. You are magical and you don't even know it. You may create anything and you are so unaware of this ability, this capability. I will now tell you that you are the most Supreme Being! You are God in a body. It's like taking part of God and putting it in a bottle. You are bottled magic and creativity and you have yet to recognize your true identity.

You will find that your true identity has been hidden beneath your judgments and low self-esteem. Once we clear your low self-worth we will be on our way to uncovering you...

God you. So, as we begin our task of uncovering your buried identity, you will find that it is necessary to stop piling on more garbage. We must dig you, the true you, out from under self-hate and self-loathing and self-deprecation. First we must stop the input of any energy that is angry or revengeful. Anger is always dense and revenge always brings punishment in the way of energy to you. Stop any anger at anyone or anything. Begin to allow everyone and everything to be in existence without "your" condemnation. Your condemnation affects you personally as it runs through your body and it puts you down into the lower, slower energies of self-loathing and low self-worth.

When you let go of your need, or addiction, to anger and revenge, you will begin to release these energies. They will then float to the surface of your cells and you will be a allowed to feel them as they leave. Do not judge you when you release anger and revenge energy. You may feel the need to yell at the world or to beat someone up. In these cases, it is best to yell into a pillow or beat on your bed. Do not act out on others as it may create other energy complications for you. You may also purchase a punching bag or stuffed bear that you can slap around. This will assist in the bodies need to release trapped anger. You all have trapped anger in your cells. I can guarantee you that if you are living in a human body; you do carry anger in your cells.

So, this is a time to clean you out with the least little effort and the greatest benefit to you. You may also use other techniques which are available to support groups, but this beating up pillows and your bed is simplest and easily accomplished right at home.

When you begin to move into a higher position of awareness, it will become easier for you to recognize when you are clearing energy. Normally you will feel that others are somehow dumber than you or maybe just not as acceptable to society as you. You may find others to be arrogant and unkind in some way. Know that when you are thinking these thoughts, you are actually piling on to all of your dense energy instead of releasing it. So, basically you are holding "you" down in low self-esteem.

Now; when you are a member of what is considered a minority group, you may have a great deal of emotional pain attached to your anger. This causes you to see life from a victim perspective and will often draw situations to you that put you down lower in your self-esteem. Please do not be angry or upset if you came into this life as a minority. You chose this role to play for a reason. Maybe in a past life you were the perpetrator and bullied or abused a person you did not feel was as worthy as you. This often occurs where you experience both roles to feel what they might be like, or how they might be overcome, or even just to see what it feels like from each perspective character. Remember – this is all just play acting and role playing, so you might try acting your way to the top and out of any victim feelings. You get to create and experience your creations just as your other soul friends now hiding in a body get to do. You are God just as everyone else is God.

Once you get the hang of accepting who you truly are, it will be easier to rise above all situations that may occur. Always know that you are going up, and always remind yourself that to go up, you must let go of all the thoughts and beliefs that might bring you down. You may lighten your load by not adding more dense energy to you. Lighten up and rise up to love!

$\mathcal{W}$ill you ever return to *homeostasis? Yes – you will become all that you once were and it is doable in this lifetime.

You have been wandering around in the desert long enough. It is time now to wake up to your true nature and to love. It is time now to be love. Let go of your fears and simply accept! Do not judge, do not fear. Be you, your true identity, by allowing this part of you to surface. You have hidden your true self for so long and now it is time to rise above all that judgment and criticism and condemnation that you are buried under.

Once you begin to release your need to judge yourself by judging others, you will feel much lighter and much freer. You will know peace, and with peace will come calm and tranquility. How would it be to feel calm and at peace no matter what occurs? How would it feel to be confident in your choices and decisions? How wonderful would it be to "know" without figuring everything out? How wonderful to simply be at peace with your feelings? No more anger, no more fear, no more confusion and no more sorrow. You will simply "know" that all is well and all will continue to be well.

Think of all the times in your life when you were confused and afraid and worried about possible "what ifs." No more "what ifs" of a negative sort please? Now you will begin to see a positive future and this will draw to you, or build a bigger, more positive future for you. Your love is in your body and you may create from love instead of fear. You may begin to ride the positivity train and get off that negativity train that you currently ride. It is only a choice away. You may focus on whatever you choose. Do you want to see the negative or do you want to see the positive? I am telling you that it is possible today, right now. Begin today and you will start to see the benefits. Your mind will calm. You will sleep better. Your dreams will improve. Your health will improve. Your entire perspective on life will improve and you will make your soul, your God persona, very, very happy. When you are that happy your vibration rises through the roof. You will no longer feel high blood pressure from stress (which is a direct result of fear), you will now feel peaceful and calm, and this will allow you to emit peace and calm energy into your world and your life.

You control the amount of peace and calm in your world. Send copious amounts if you wish. Flood your world and your life with love. Be you. Be strong in love and you will be adding so much light to the world by "emitting" great amounts of light to the world. You affect everyone around you simply by loving you. Do yourself a favor and give the world a great big gift. Love you. Nurture you. Heal you!

*Note: Sometimes I channel words and am unsure of their meaning. When I first started channeling God's books I used my mom's old 1946 Webster's Dictionary to look up definitions. These days I use the internet.

Homeostasis: "Homeostasis is the ability to maintain a relatively stable internal state that persists despite changes in the world outside…"

– LiveScience.com   *Liane*

꧁꧂

You have always been a soul, a spirit, a being of light. You will never end and you will always come and go at will.

You have been the most intelligent and the highest vibration there is. You only dim your light in order to enter this material world that you so love to play in. It is like your childhood game of *Pin the Tail on the Donkey.* You must first get blindfolded; then you must spin around until you are dizzy. It is how you enter or begin the game. In this case you must go dumb and blind to who you truly are. It would not be fun to be completely aware of who you are and to the fact that you never end. You would not feel the importance of emotions and of insight.

When you are God (All That Is) you are aware that you are eternal and you are aware that you exist forever. Why not have some fun with it and pretend that you do not exist forever? And while you're at it, why not pretend that you do not know everything and that you are even unaware that you are God? It is as though you went to a show where a hypnotist was entertaining, and this hypnotist asked for volunteers who might enjoy the feeling of being hypnotized and made to believe they were someone else... a king maybe or maybe a baby crying. This hypnotist could take you to a new or different level of consciousness or awareness, and you would truly believe them when they told you to act like a king or to act like a baby.

You are under the influence of hypnosis, and you are freaking out and believing everything that you "think" you see. And the reason you "see" it is because you are thinking it! Change your mind... see it differently. Let go of your need to frighten yourself to keep you in line and safe. You need not frighten a child with death if they cross the busy street without holding your hand. You need not use threats to train your children and you need not use threats to train yourself. You have been programmed to believe in punishment and retribution. It is time to let the old programming go. You may rise above the need for self-punishment to keep you in line. You may rise above the need for a punishing God. You have been taught to fear God simply to keep you in line and obeying the rules.

You have come up from superstition and it is time now to set yourself free. Fear has held you down and love will set you free. You will walk this earth and know love by letting go of fear. You let go of fear by seeing everything differently. Begin to see everything from love (acceptance) and you will create a huge shift for yourself from fear to love. Love brings you up in vibration. You may heal yourself with love, love is all it takes. Allow everything to be what it is without judging it and you will turn the corner. Then begin to find some small thing that is good in everyone and everything. Look for the good in it and you will be turning you in a whole new direction. You will begin to move towards your good and away from bad and awful.

Do you think that life is awful? Do you think that people are awful? Do you have a hard time loving life and accepting life? Begin to "see" it differently by "thinking" differently. Your mind will lead you if you just tell it where to go and what to look for. Look for the good. Find the good. Make this your new game. Find good in everything even war. How? Decide that no one ever dies and that souls are playing at fighting with other soul friends, but they are really shadow boxing and going out of this three dimensional world and coming back in. They may want to play a new and different role, but the only way to do that is to leave the stage and reenter in a whole new costume.

You may find it difficult to believe from where you now stand in your blindfolded, dizzy, unaware state, but this is what you are dealing with. You are deaf, dumb and blind and you are trying to find your way around. You may begin to see clearly by taking off your blindfold and looking for love. Love is all around you if you will just focus on it!

✺

*U*ou have lost your sense of humor. Most often you cannot see the fun and games in life. When you live from fear, you begin to take everything so seriously. You forget how to be flexible and you begin to close yourself off to all the possibilities of life.

When you are a child, you are open to all possibilities. For the most part, children are unafraid unless they have been born with connected energy from a past life. Often children remember past lives for a short time and then those memories begin to fade. If you have such memories, you more than likely do not share them with others.

So; in childhood you are, for the most part, unafraid and adventurous. You are then taught what to fear and what to trust. The trust part of life is very limited and the fear part is quite large. As you fear more, you begin to draw more of what you fear. In the same vein, as you trust more, you begin to draw more of what you trust. The problem you seem to have with trust is that it doesn't seem to last. Even if you put your trust in your parents, they may have let you down and disappointed you. "Trust must be earned" is a very big belief among you. Now I would like you to begin to trust. Trust your soul. Trust that you are being guided and watched over and loved beyond measure. Trust that you... spirit/soul you... is always in your corner and always has your back.

Some of you believe strongly in angels to guide and protect you. This is advantageous and is often confused with protection from others or from horrific events. In actuality angels, or guides, do exist and have always existed. You have many parts of you that you are totally and completely unaware of at this time. Once you begin to realize how looked after and loved and watched over you truly are, you will begin to feel a little safer in life. As you feel safer, you will let go of some of your insecurities.

One of your biggest problems is not trusting yourself. Depending on how strict your upbringing was, you may think that you never do anything right and that you are very ignorant and mistake prone. This type of thinking is common and often it is followed by the assumption that everyone is stupid and mistake prone. You have been taught to believe that mistakes are bad and that success is based on doing everything right. Mistakes are not bad or wrong. When things do not go your way it is a way of showing you how flexible you may be. When you are flexible you are capable of change, and with change comes your evolution.

You are evolving! You are constantly evolving and growing and expanding and, as you do so, you begin to see how a new way might enhance your life. You must learn to change as you grow, simply because you are becoming something or someone new. You are becoming more of your true self which is light and love, and you are letting go of the old, fearful, dense self. It is not a mistake to take on light and let go of fear. Also, it was not a mistake to take on fear and the density required to get a good root system in this dense dimension of materiality. This material world requires a strong, solid energy to match it. It is like drilling down in order to get a good foothold or root system going. Then you may rise up to a higher level without losing your hold on the third dimension until you are ready for the fourth and fifth and so on.

You came in as you did for a reason. You began to grow roots just like a plant and now it is time to rise above the soil and to bloom and grow higher. You are growing and changing and this was the plan. Trust everything that got you here and trust your choices. Trust that there is something much greater than this unconscious you who is still working in the dark, and know that you are watched over and guided. You are doing well and you are right where you wanted to be at this particular time. You have done well and you are right on schedule. Nothing went wrong and your plan was/is a success. You are "in" and now you are learning how to "rise" above to the next step. Good job! Well done!

∾⧉∾

Once in a while I am able to contact you on earth. You have a great deal of fear where God is concerned and so this is no easy task. After all, what would you do if you heard a big voice that came from everywhere and said it was God?

This was the case for Liane. She was originally contacted by her soul and she spent a little over a year communicating with and getting to know that part of herself. Soul communication is a little more common than God communication. It is really unique for humans but is considered normal for spirit. Whenever spirit, or soul, or other energy beings, get the opportunity to cross dimensions and communicate, it is quite well received by such spirits and beings. This is due to the fact that it is not such an easy form of communication. Most humans are taught and trained to avoid the unknown and to communicate only with human beings and to ignore spirit beings. This causes a great deal of separation between the material plane and the spiritual plane.

So; once you lose a loved one, you are not allowed to communicate with them. This, of course, is not a rule, it is only a fear put in place long ago. Fear of the unknown is very, very big on earth and you all freak out over the thought of ghosts and paranormal activity. This is not the way you really would like to live and most of you would enjoy a good talk with your own soul, or spirit, that guides you from within. Can you imagine being afraid of a part of yourself? Can you imagine the separation this creates within the self? Can you imagine being told you have a soul but must not speak with this part of you? Can you imagine living in a world where you are told you must not communicate with anyone who does not wear a body?

Angels are among you and you are told it is okay to ask them for help and protection and even intuitive guidance; however, you must never hear them. You also must never hear God or your soul. You may only speak and never listen to or hear their voices. Fear of the unknown is so great among you that you may only read about others who venture into these unknown territories. You may or may not believe their stories and their communications; however you may read about those who communicate with spirit. You may not, however, believe in those communications, so you do not speak freely about your belief in them for fear of frightening your friends. After all, it is not good to hear voices and you may be considered crazy. It is good to hear from God directly in your prayers but it is crazy to actually hear God talk to you. You may talk to God, but God may not talk to you. You may be considered crazy to even "think" you hear God. And then, of course, we have a great deal of stigma attached to hearing any voices that are not coming from a body.

So; with all of these beliefs, how do you expect to ever receive information from your own soul? You are not a body with a soul! You are a soul who came to earth and must wear a body to get in! How in the world will soul ever communicate with body and mind if the mind is telling body to be afraid of your own soul, or who you really are? You are in quite a pickle and I am here to show you a way out – you may simply write to your soul and your soul may write to you. This is how Liane began her communication… here is her story:

A dear friend invited Liane and about twenty friends to her home to hear a psychic channel. Liane had read about Edgar Cayce who was quite famous and so she looked forward to this event. Also, this event occurred at a time when a great deal of light was entering this dimension, allowing for humans to be a little more open to the other dimensions. So, this event was quite small and the psychic channel was a lovely lady who spoke about her training in England and how she channeled a spirit energy group. She began by talking about this energy group and how one day the group asked her to write a dream book. The psychic wasn't crazy about the idea of automatic writing, but agreed to allow her energy group to channel or write their dream book through her. She said that she finally sat down and wrote, "Is anyone there?" This began her written communication with her energy group and she completed a dream book for them.

The psychic then went on to answer questions from the group of twenty or so who had gathered. The next morning Liane went to her pool to get some sun. As I told you, she had read about Edgar Cayce and had learned about the importance of dreams and how they were your subconscious way of getting information to you. Because she wanted to translate her dream from the night before she grabbed her pencil and notebook to take to the pool with her.

Once at the pool, she took out her rather large notebook and her pencil. For some strange reason, the only thing she could think about was what the psychic had said the night before, i.e., that she finally sat down and wrote "Is anyone there?" so Liane wrote "Is anyone there?" and put her pencil on the page of paper and almost dared it to move. And it did! A great big giant "YES" was printed on lines about five or six lines high.   Liane was so surprised! She had never experienced anything like it before. She looked down at her body as she sat in her beach chair and she literally thought, "Oh shit – there's someone in here!" Her words, not mine! She then wrote, "Who are you?" and received a name.   She knew she was not consciously writing and she was (in her words) "blown away" by the whole experience.

This began a very loving and long relationship with spirit. Because she was strongly programmed by religion, she was not told right away that she channeled her soul. She was led to believe that she was communicating with a spirit guide, which was easier for her to assimilate since she had read about Edgar Cayce. She was later (about a year later), exposed to the big giant voice of God. I came in at that time in her training to get her accustomed to the "idea" that humans may communicate directly with God and to teach her that God is not exactly what man has painted God to be. This has been an ongoing process and slowly, over time, she has let go of some of her more fearful ideas about God. She is free now to love and appreciate God/Source/All That Is without fear and superstition regarding the unknown.

This is what I want for you. I want you to have freedom from your fear of God and of your soul. You live in you and yet you (mind you) are afraid of you. You are superstitious and afraid because you have been trained and taught and programmed. Now it is time to rise above such nonsense and to realize that your fears of the unknown are holding you down.

Now; if all this talk of spirits and energy beings is too much for you and frightens you further, it is due to the fact that you are ready to release some of these dense fears. Your fears must come to the surface in order for you to heal and to lighten your load. You are only healing and you are growing in awareness. Liane has channeled my writings for over thirty-five years and it has only assisted her in her life. She is never told what to do and everything is always done with great respect and gratitude and regard for her free will choices. You too are allowed to make your free will choices. You may ignore any information given here and you will still be wonderful and amazing. Choices are only that... it's all just a choice. You may go left or you may go right or you may stay right where you are. It's all good!

⁂

$\mathcal{I}$t has been a long time since you on earth have been in contact with your spiritual guides and angels and other forms. At one time on earth, it was very common to find those who consulted their higher self on daily matters. Today this seems strange to you and is quite obsolete.

Well, now is a good time to reconnect with you. Now is the perfect time to go within. You spend all of your time focusing on the outer world which is only a reflection of what is "in" you. You will find that your outer world changes when you begin to change inside. When you change your mind about things, things in your life seem different. When you decide to let go of your anger at an individual and no longer wish to seek revenge on them in the way of punishment, you will be turning a very big corner and this will cause a big "shift" within you. You will see how easy it is to let go of harsh feelings and this may prompt you to let go of even greater amounts of harsh, dense energy.

Say you have a family member whom you have always had issues with in the past. Maybe this family member is a sibling and you simply cannot understand how they can be so wrong in their behavior. In this particular case it does not matter what the behavior is because we all know by now that wrong behavior does not exist. So, what is it that so upsets you about this sibling? It could be that you are not in control of their behavior and you feel that their behavior reflects poorly on you or on your family. Family dynamics are quite interesting and usually, on a soul level, you have requested your very best soul friends to come in and be a part of your earth family. These soul friends have often shared many past lives with you, and they are the ones you most depend on to help you experience what you wish to learn in life. This life is just one of many that you may have experienced with them.

When you come into a life (or movie role), you do so usually with great enthusiasm. In this case, you may be in agreement with your soul friend to assist you in being flexible and more God like in your earth life. Often you, as soul, come to earth with the intent to bring in more light awareness. Often you wish to assist this dimension in some way, and you wish also to experience feelings and the five senses that are so prevalent here on earth. You may wish to have a peaceful life, or you may wish to put blocks in your way of a peaceful life, to see how long it takes you to achieve your goal of rising to a peaceful life. You may be playing a game with yourself just as you play games in human life. Sometimes your game, your entertainment, is based on achieving a new level in your game.

Souls play! That's what they do! They cross dimensions and they pop in and out of dimensions and they have fun because they are light! They are you and you are them. Please lighten up and begin to see that you are playing a part. Right now many of you are playing the part of a frightened, angry person. You are not the role that you are playing, and you may easily drop your attitude and lighten up and get very flexible in your mind. Your thoughts are scaring you and holding you down. Let go of all negative beliefs about good and bad or right and wrong. Move over to... "Everything is okay, and if I do not like the way things are I can simply walk away." You are strongly taught on earth to hold tight to family and stay connected to family. This may work in most situations; however, I can assure you that it is okay to leave any abusive situation. Also, be aware that you cannot fix anyone, and often it is best to allow them to live the life, and experience the situations, that they (as a soul) came to earth to experience.

When it comes to family, as with anyone else on the planet, you are not responsible for their behavior, and you sometimes are meant to walk away... no hate... no revenge... no responsibility. Rules are all made up by you depending on what you have chosen to believe. You are the creator of your reality, and you may choose to forgive and let go... "let go and let God" is another very good axiom. Let go and trust in a higher power. If you are meant to be in someone's life you will be. You cannot lose. You are always where you are meant to be and you are experiencing what you came to experience. Sometimes you even learn and grow out of specific experiences, and you often rise above the chaos and conflict to peacefulness.

Peace is within just as everything is within. Go within my friends. Contact your soul. Learn about life from a higher perspective. Learn how to love you by accepting your own God self. Your soul is a very loving part of you and will guide you well. Trust your guidance and you will begin to calm your anger. You are angry at them because you do not trust you! When you trust you, you will let go of your fear of "what ifs" and you will calm down and find your peace.

*Y*ou will find that as you connect more and more with the idea that you are a spiritual being, you will begin to see life in a whole new way. Life will become more of an adventure just as it was in childhood. You will wake to a new day with enthusiasm and wonder. You will wonder what good thing awaits you and what gifts might come your way. You will feel the innocence of childhood, as you will no longer be judging yourself or others. You will be free of criticism and self-punishment. You will love and accept yourself just as you are.

You didn't know that you could dig yourself into such a hole just by focusing on the negatives, and your sense of freedom will bring you great joy. It will feel like you have been living in a cave and now you have set yourself free to see daylight. You will feel refreshed and energetic and you will thrive in your freedom. You are a free spirit and you will literally be setting you free. It only requires a shift in perception and awareness. It only takes moving to your center. It only takes acceptance and love.

You are moving in a very good-for-you direction. You are moving into the positive energy and away from the negative energy. It is like cleaning yourself off and moving out of the mud that you have been looking at and immersing yourself in. You will come into the light and out of the darkness of your muddy, dark cave. You will be lighter and your life will feel easier and it will flow for you. Actually, you will be the one who is flowing but it will feel like life has given you this gift. You are the one who gives and takes from you. You are the one who decides what to call bad. You may choose a better or more efficient way of creating. Simply let your soul free. Let the love and light in you free. Let acceptance take over for a while. You have been rejecting life long enough. Try to embrace all the good around you. You cannot see the good if you are busy focusing on the bad and looking for things to go wrong. You only get more of what you search for just like on your computers. It is a reflection of how you are programming yourself.

Feed yourself love and light and joy and positivity. Stop looking for the downfall of others, for you are causing you to fall. The fall of man is being brought on by man, simply because he/she does not realize that he/she is a great big creating machine. You may change how you create. Look for the good! Look for the light! Look for the joy and happiness. Watch funny and fun movies and shows. Read loving and light articles. Would you feed a baby horror stories or murder mysteries? No – I don't think you would. Why? Simply because a baby would think it was "real." Well, your body, your cells, your nervous system does not know the difference between what is real and what is perceived. You are feeding you fear. Come over to love!

⁂

*Y*ou have a fondness for drama. You require high levels of drama and conflict if you have been feeding yourself drama and conflict. Be careful what you feed yourself and look at how you (your mind) respond to what you are taking in.

If you wish for peace and contentment, it is a good idea to turn towards peace and contentment. Do not force yourself to take "in" the chaos if you do not wish to live in chaos. You may release your own chaos by moving closer to peace. When you are at peace, you do not get sucked into the arguments and disagreements of others. You maintain your hold on peace and you maintain your position in the center – your center. When you are centered, you do not easily get riled up and you do not lose your cool. When you are centered, you live in your own personal reality of peace and you do not give your peaceful energy away for a challenge. When you live in peace, your peaceful energy will surround you and you will not feel the urge to move towards conflict.

Peacefulness is a very calm and happy state of being. Peacefulness requires calm and tranquility. You do not achieve your peace by arguing with your friends and neighbors over your differences. You achieve peace by accepting diversity and by allowing all ideas and truths to exist. This is a big one, actually a very big one, for you to digest. You all want to put your personal spin on things and you all want to be on top of any given situation or debate. You hate to lose and your ego does not want to be wrong. Your ego fears being wrong because it means you may be punished. In childhood, you are often punished for wrongdoing and so this programming is often strong in you.

So, my advice to you is to allow yourself to be wrong. Allow yourself to not always be right. Allow yourself to be flexible enough to move out of your current position and closer to your center. You will not lose if you move closer to peace. You will not lose if you give up your position and collapse into unknowingness. You need not pretend to have all the answers and you may wish to surrender and move into love (acceptance) and allow yourself to move out of chaos and control.

You have no idea how creating really works and it, this lack of awareness, is causing you to assume that control is your answer. Well, the opposite is true – surrender may be your best choice. Move to higher awareness by letting go of your current beliefs. Your current beliefs tell you to keep a strong control over everything that you fear. This causes a big imbalance of energy and now it is time to let go of your control and trust that all is going to be okay. Allow everything to be okay until you can move up in your beliefs to allow everything to be good.

Allow yourself to accept your good by allowing for a better way. You may allow for a better way by "choosing" to let go and let God take over.

Do not search your Internet for right answers that uphold your current beliefs or your current standing. If you are trying to rise above the chaos, do not focus on and send you (your energy) into the chaos. You may rise above any and all situations in this way. Preserve your peace by showing you peace and calm and acceptance. Do not worry about what the rest of the world is focusing on. You may break away and move from war and chaos to peace. Your breaking away and looking a new direction will help others to break away, simply because you are all energy beings and you are all connected. It is time now to rise above your human nature into your spiritual nature. Spirit knows it is all smoke and mirrors and that you are only dreaming this whole thing up. Spirit will guide you home to you... to love... to light. Be spiritual in nature. Give up the need for chaos and begin to choose peace.

First, one falls away from war then another and another, until everyone is moving over to peace. Oh what a wonderful game that you play, and you have no idea how powerful you are.

⚘

*Y*ou have always wanted peace and love because you are a peaceful, loving being. When you are at war you do not do well. Chaos is a form of struggle and survival. When you let go of your need to disagree and to show how right you are, or how brilliant you think you are, you will move closer to peace. Fighting and arguing is a direct reflection of anger, and all anger comes from fear. Fear, as we have determined, is the opposite of love.

If I were to tell you to love your neighbor, you would think that I mean you should invite them to dinner or over for tea. This is not what I mean. When I say "please love your neighbor," I mean live and let live, accept as is, allow for differences but do not allow for abusive behavior. When you attack one another, you are basically attacking part of you. It is like a cancer cell attacking the body it lives in. When you feel attacked or threatened, you feel the need to attack back. This is a learned and taught behavior. When it comes to attack, your ego is involved and you also go into survival mode. Most of you evolved through history fighting to survive and fighting to move forward; and now you simply fight for your beliefs and some of you fight because you are "afraid" of another's beliefs.

It is time to stop all war and to come out of your fears. You believe some groups to be dangerous because of their beliefs and this is also due to fear. When you move from fear to love, you, as a species, will no longer have the will to fight. You will begin to understand cause and effect, and you will begin to see how you create it all simply by thinking it into being. Please stop thinking fearful thoughts, as you are creating more fear by doing so; and fear only leads to more anger and anger always leads to greater chaos and war. There is never war without fear and consequently anger. You may stop war by letting go of fear of "what ifs"... "what if this goes wrong" or "what if they do this" or "what if they are lying and we suffer for it" and even "what if I'm not smart enough to see the danger that lies ahead?" These fears are causing you to become afraid, angry, hostile and very, very nervous. You have headaches and problems with your nervous system and depression and even cancer. Something is eating at you and it is fear. Fear is the strongest of the denser energies and so I am addressing this issue today. You do not like fear and you do not enjoy reading about fear. It is time now to switch from fear to love, and you cannot do that if you continue to always go into fearful evaluation on every situation that is occurring on your planet.

World events are not your responsibility. You do not need to solve all the world's problems and you are far too sensitive and emotional in your evaluations of life on earth at this time. You do not need to control everything and you do not need to be aware of everything that is going on outside of you. That is only "your" reflection. You change the outer reflection by changing you. Chaos within reflects in your mirror as chaos and war. Please, please stop scaring yourself and begin to trust that all will be well. Trust that there is a higher power and that everything is really in good hands. Trust that life will continue as always and trust that you came here to play a role and you do not explode and disappear into oblivion. You are never-ending. You do not end. You simply go back to Source and you catch your breath, and you turn right around and you jump back into this earth pool once again. You love it and you do it often.

So, why tremble in fear and lose your health to anger? Why stress those billions and trillions of cells and atoms in your personal body when this is just a game? Why see the worst when you can see the best? It is all illusion! Do you want your hair to turn gray and fall out? Do you want your body bombarded with stress hormones? Stress hormones slow your immune system and happy hormones, like dopamine, strengthen your immune system. Stay happy... let go of anger and fearful thoughts... come over to trust and peace and "everything will be okay." Let go of all other thoughts regarding your future. "Everything will be okay!"

❧

*Y*ou are very slow when it comes to absorbing specific kinds of information. This causes you to turn to a new way of thinking, slowly and more deliberately.

Most of you require repetition to learn. You are stuck in one way of seeing life on earth and you require being told over and over again how you may change. Because of this, I use a great deal of repetition to help you move forward in your thinking. So, today I will remind you that you live in your own personal reality bubble. It is like a sphere of energy around you and you are constantly filling it with your thoughts, ideas and beliefs, in the form of energy. So; as I mentioned earlier, it is like filling up a balloon to bursting. You may fill your balloon with thoughts of love, peace and happiness or you may fill your balloon to bursting with fear, hate and unloving feelings of all kinds. Every time you have a thought you put air (ideas) into your balloon and you get to walk around in it all day.

The best way for you to handle this situation is to constantly focus on love, peace and happiness. Any thought or idea that will bring you into love, peace or happiness will do. If you accidentally think unloving, unkind thoughts about your enemies (all enemies are only perceived), I want you to think two or three loving thoughts to balance your energy to the direction of love, peace and happiness. You may blow up your reality big with love and this will assist you in living in love. The same is true for happiness and peace. Please learn to focus on what you want for yourself. You live in your energy. You "are" energy and energy affects and moves energy into new directions and territories. Where do you want your energy to take you? Where are you sending you?

⚛

*Y*ou have always been a loving energy force and you have always been creative in nature. Now it is time to remember who you are and to live up to your full potential. You may do this by letting go of your fear, and you let go of fear by seeing all differently. This is why I tell you to look for the good that is all around you. If you constantly focus on the things you don't like, those things will begin to take over your thoughts and you will find yourself disgusted with everyone and everything. When you are in negative thinking, you may become frustrated with people and with life. On the other hand, when you are focusing on, and thinking of, the positive ideas, you will become very happy with life. It's just that simple. Focus on positive and your mind moves your body and your energy into happy. Focus on negative and you get moved into frustration and anger and worry and concern and, ultimately, into fear.

You may live your life in fear or you may live your life in joy and love. It's so simple once you get the hang of it – negative thoughts bring negative reactions, and positive thoughts bring positive reactions to you. Negative equals negative, and positive equals positive. You get to choose. You get to create "for" you! You may give you joy and happiness, or you may give you upset and unhappiness. You create it and you decide it by your choice of perspective.

So; leave your creative energy up to you and do not blame what you see, or how you see it, on anyone else. Not many of you realize how you create your own view of the world, and those who do, have become more of an observer and less of a judge. So; let go of fear and you will begin to shift over to the love side of you. Let go of your need to judge and to criticize and you will move into acceptance, and acceptance will lead to peace of mind. Peace of mind will calm your body, and your emotions will fall into balance. Peace of mind will bring more peaceful energy to you and you will one day find yourself living in heaven right here on earth. You will have brought heaven to earth simply by using your creative power.

You choose where you live. You may decide that you enjoy heaven on earth and you may decide that living in a world of chaos and fear is not for you. Be brave enough to become an explorer of this new world. You may break away from the pack (those who choose to continue to view negativity) and venture into this new world of peace and love. When you make this "choice" to rise above to the next dimension, you will be assisting others and blazing a new trail. Just as any adventurer who has scouted new lands, you will be opening a door that will get wider and wider as more people awaken and choose to move into love and away from fear.

You can do this! Others have already opened the door for you and you only need to walk through to the other side. Do not be afraid to leave this third dimension that is based on duality. Do not be afraid to move up and out of chaos. Do not be afraid to be more than you now are. Do not be afraid to be love and acceptance.

You are rising above this dimension in an effort to move into the fourth and on to the fifth dimension of light and love. Don't stop now... you've got a good start. Fear is leaving and judgment is becoming a thing of the past. You are moving up to love and you will most enjoy it; and you will rejoice in the fact that you can and will create a beautiful heaven right here on earth... "Thy kingdom come, thy will be done, on earth as it is in heaven."

≈⋓≈

*Y*ou will have no problem believing that you mess up in life, because you have been taught to believe that you make big mistakes. What if you are doing exactly what was planned by your soul? What if you are moving and expressing just as your soul planned, in order to get specific responses, in order to learn how to move in this material world? What if you do not make huge mistakes and what if everything you have ever experienced has led you to this desire to rise "up?" Maybe everything happens for a reason and maybe you actually are right where you are meant to be.

Ascension is a process of rising above one dimension to the next. If you are satisfied with where you are, you usually will not wish to leave where you are. It takes wanting and searching for more information in order to receive new information, which can bring greater insight and awareness to you. Once you lived in total darkness and were completely unaware that you had any connection to nature and others on your planet. You may have relatives that you do not know are related to you until you are told. DNA analysis will reveal your true parents to you and also your true siblings. So, does it really matter if you live with those who are genetically connected? No – it does not. You may grow into adulthood in your current family and then discover that you were adopted and have no real blood connection to them.

So – is family most important simply because you are connected genetically or is it because you feel responsibility and gratitude towards them? If you were adopted and then met your true parents, would you feel strongly connected to these true parents because you came from them, or would you continue to feel connected to your newly discovered adoptive parents? Do we love out of nurture or do we love out of DNA connection? Do we see family as most important because we are related or do we see family as most important because they were there in our formative years?

It is quite apparent that those who take good care of you will feel good to you and those who ignore you will not feel that close. So; who is most important to your survival? Does it matter if a stranger who is not connected by bloodline takes care of you or if your true blood parent takes care of you? You get to choose and you get to decide. Do not be concerned if you have been separated from your bloodline family. Do not fear that you are somehow disconnected and lost. You choose before you enter earth who you wish to live with, and you actually request other soul friends to be your parents and to play other roles for you.

Do you have a parent who abandoned you and gave you up for adoption? This may have been your plan before you entered earth. You may have set up agreements with many different soul friends to play many different roles in your life. Some "you" agreed to play roles for and others agree to play roles "for" you. So, how can you judge what you do not understand and what you are totally unaware of? How can you decide that you have made mistakes when you do not know what your plans were before coming here to earth? And how can you judge others for the role they have played in your life when you may have been the one who requested that they play this role for you?

You are always on your path to growing and evolving; only you do not realize that you are. And if you do realize that you are on your evolutionary path, you do not consciously know what will get you there. So why not allow your life and your path to unfold for you and not get too involved in trying to control everything? When the plan, any plan, is unknown it might be a good idea to sit back and watch and see what happens next. You don't know what plan you made with your current family and you don't know (unless you have been DNA tested) if your true family is out there somewhere. And if your true family is out there somewhere, might they be the strangers you are judging right now? If you could be related to anyone and not be aware of it, might you be judging your true family out of ignorance? And if you are related to everyone, who is left to judge?

Please let go of your need to judge others, as all "others" are not only related to you, you are the same "energy being" expressing through matter. You come from the same source and you are the same energy, simply expressing in a different way. You are one giant God force moving through matter and expressing through matter. Your family "is" you too, and strangers "are" you too. Give up the idea that only family matters. You are all one giant soul family who come and go from this dimension; and I guarantee you that the stranger who is far away in a strange land, using customs that are confusing and strange to you, is your dear lost soul friend. You are all family and you do not know that you are.

◈

You have always been love, you have always been light and you have always been energy. You often see yourself as clumsy and awkward and this is due to the fact that you are living in matter. You actually live and breathe in the material world that you have created. It is as though you created a world and then you entered this world of created matter. It would be like blowing a giant bubble and then popping into your bubble to live.

If you could enter your bubble in order to experience what is there, don't you think you might be capable of exiting your bubble or popping back out? Yes – you have this capability and this creative ability. You may simply shift your focus and rise above your bubble. Simply turn off the noise and go within. Use your meditative skills to rise above to the next level and begin to see a whole new view. Calm your nerves and silence your concerns and simply pretend that everything is blissful until you can rise to blissful feelings.

Everything that affects you is based on how you perceive it and how you respond to it. When you respond with stress and anger, you receive greater stress and possibly rage. You do not receive rage or anger or stress if you do not respond in that manner. If you stay calm and maybe even think of something else, your emotions will respond to your response. Your emotions ride up and down with your thoughts. If you respond with negative thoughts your emotions go to a negative, dense place. On the other hand, if you respond with a positive thought, your emotions rise to a lighter response. You control it all by how you choose to respond to any daily situation. Respond with calmness and you turn any stressful event into a possible peaceful and maybe even helpful event.

You are the catalyst! You are the one who turns simple, ignorant and often abusive statements into something big and explosive or something small and meaningless. You decide if you want to make someone into a villain for making abusive statements or if you wish to retain peace of mind and allow that person to be someone who simply needs help. You decide how your movie will play out and how awful your personal reality may feel or how good your personal reality will feel.

You may search high and low for things to complain about or you may see from a new perspective. If you find yourself constantly complaining about those you perceive to be villains, you may wish to go within and look at your wounds. Usually a wounded person who is in pain will require help rising above victimhood. Those who constantly find villains, or people who are unfair to them, are sometimes playing a victim role. When you feel vulnerable from your past wounds, you may see the world as harsh and insensitive to your needs. You may be unaware of childhood wounds (or even past life wounds), which can lead you to be overly sensitive and overly protective in nature. In this case you may find yourself constantly searching for a safe place to exist.

You are what is commonly referred to as the walking wounded and your emotional body needs to come into balance. You may assist in your own healing by realizing that you have an overblown need for protection and so you do not trust life at all. You are wounded and you are waiting for the next betrayal or attack. You spend your time trying to avoid pitfalls and danger. You may avoid certain types of people and situations in an effort to protect yourself and to keep you safe. You may have high moral opinions and these beliefs allow you to sit in a position of self-righteousness. It allows you to feel good about yourself if you happen to carry a great deal of shame from specific types of wounds.

Sexual behavior has a great deal of judgment placed against it and those who believe they have been sexually abused will have a great deal of shame due to these judgments. When you have been sexually abused, you may require professional help. You also may assist yourself by writing to your soul or just writing to yourself. You may sit down and write, "Why am I angry" and then place your pen back on the paper and wait for it to move. This technique is common and is often used to assist you in moving those trapped emotions. It is a technique of writing to yourself in order to receive your own answers.

If this technique does not appeal to you, you may wish to try hypnosis. Find yourself a broadminded hypnotherapist who will take you back to any sexual or other type of abuse that may be affecting your emotional body at this time. You may receive answers from childhood or from past lives. Either way it is cause and effect at work. A wound is a wound and it does not matter where in time it came from. I specifically bring up sexual abuse because it is quite common, as sex is so misunderstood and often judged as bad and sinful. This, of course, is ridiculous and totally uncalled for. Sex is fun and man has turned it into something big and dangerous and forbidden. It's difficult to talk to you about sex because you have so many restrictions regarding sex. Mostly you fear sex and you fear your own bodies because you were taught shame. Shame is a byproduct of guilt and guilt will bring you down.

When you have great guilt you pretend to be someone you are not. When you have great guilt, you actually draw some type of punishment to yourself. You must release this guilt that you all carry. Not everyone has been sexually abused but pretty much everyone carries some type of sexual guilt from living in a body that has sex. You live in a body that is identified by its sexuality. You are all concerned about boy babies and girl babies. You all want to know "is it a girl or is it a boy?" and then you subscribe certain characteristics to each, depending on the sex of the child. Now we are beginning to create greater judgment against sex by judging homosexuals and those who are gender fluid. It is all okay! Let go of this need to judge and to be afraid of your bodies. This is ridiculous. Let it all go. God is totally okay with whatever you choose to do with your body. God loves you and accepts you just as you are. You are playing with your creative abilities and having fun. Continue to love you no matter what. Do not fall prey to judgment and guilt. You are perfect just as you are and you are loved just as you are. You are judging you by judging them. Please rise to a higher level of understanding where sex is concerned. You are creating it all and all of it is good!

❧

*Y*ou will come to a place in your healing that is most important for you. This will be when you actually become aware that you are the creator of your reality. When you know it is all you making things look the way that you see them, you will change how you see them and you will know that you are the observer as well as the actor.

You have always wanted to be something more and now you are moving in that direction. Once you take on the role of the observer of your life, you will be free. You will accept all occurrences and you will allow your life to unfold. It will be magical for you and the fact that you no longer will be judging life will allow you to release all self-punishment. After all, self-punishment is a direct result of bringing or drawing punishment to you because you are guilty of something. When you are innocent, you no longer require punishment.

So, as you release your hold on punishment, you will begin to receive the gifts of an innocent person who is loving and kind. Why loving and kind? Simply because you will no longer carry hatred and anger and dense feelings of this nature. Remember – you are magnetic in nature and you draw to you that which you are. You draw negative when you carry negative within you and you draw positive when you carry positive within you. You will easily get the hang of this once you begin to move into positive energy and away from negative energy.

As you make this change you will find that there may be times when you are drawn back to negative thoughts. This could be due to clearing of energy that is leaving you. When you clear energy, you actually release it from your cells. You let it go from where ever in your body it has been attached. The book I mentioned earlier by Louise Hay, the *Heal Your Body* book, will allow you to see what thoughts and emotions might be carried in certain areas of your body. Knowing what energy you are clearing and releasing may be extremely helpful for some of you.

As you clear energy, you may experience pain or sluggishness. This is common as dense energy detaches and rises in you. Soreness is often caused by energy that is carried in you and you will wish to release all denseness, as it holds you down. As you rise, you literally raise your vibration and you vibrate faster. You might feel like you are getting younger and more vibrant. Then, after you have been vibrating faster for a while, you actually begin to shake loose more dense energy. It will break apart and dislodge due to your higher vibration. As it dislodges, it floats to the surface to be released and you may feel this denseness as it comes to the surface. You may feel like you are having a bad day emotionally or you may feel sluggish as I mentioned earlier.

It is all energy going. You are an energy being and you carry energy. You release and emit energy and you carry energy. This is a process of rising up and healing. Very few of you have evolved to a level of awareness where you may instantaneously rise to the next dimension. If you are wondering why your spiritual path has become emotional and difficult, it may be due to clearing and releasing energy. As you rise higher you are literally vibrating faster and the old dense energy that you have always held on to, in the way of beliefs and ideas, is leaving. The new awareness that you are taking on is causing a higher vibration to occur, which shakes things loose in your cells. Cellular memory and perception of those memories are changing and moving and letting go of their hold on you.

You are changing and growing into a new version of you. This is the New World that you are moving into. You are the new version of you and you are the world! You create your world view and your life view by how you see and then translate what you see into "your" reality bubble. You are creating a new world "in" you. You are the change that everyone is talking about. "You" are the one who is pulling back the veil of untruth, and by doing so you are revealing the truth. It's not about "them" out there. It is about "you" in here!

꙳

You will always wonder and explore and investigate because you are curious. You like to know how things work and even how you can take them apart and reassemble them. This is a time of reassembling you and changing how you see life and the world in general. You get to reassess your own ideas and beliefs, and in doing so, you get to change you and how you accept or reject parts of life.

You will find that you no longer wish to wake to a new day and feel like you must drag yourself from your bed. You may become excited about life and what you will see today and who you will meet. You will know that those you encounter are actually part of you and are connected to you. How wonderful to know that you have this connection. You will learn to appreciate the beauty of life just as it is. It is amazing how you have built cities and even governments and how you have organized and civilized your lives. You have doctors and teachers and even law officers who keep rule over you so you do not go too crazy killing and pillaging. Before you had law officers you were pretty wild with your pillaging and plundering. I know that you complain about your laws but at one time in your evolution it was a very good idea.

Everything is cause and effect, and you may not realize in advance what kind of effect some actions will have. Most of your laws were for a reason at the time and not always for a good reason. Many laws are set in place to keep order and prevent chaos. We also have laws that stop you from stealing and harming others. Do not be so quick to judge law and order. You may wish to get rid of governments who govern you and you may have strong grievances against them, but you did set them in place for a reason. Now you are ready for change and you are seeing your governments in a negative way. You do not feel looked after and taken care of; you feel more like you are bullied and you, many of you, are rebelling.

It is time now to calm down until you can come to a place where you are more peaceful. Everything that you see in your outer world is only a reflection of what is going on "inside" of you. You are a giant projector, who is projecting and emitting energy, and then you view your projections and you hate what you see. You are looking at the discord that is going on within "you." When you calm your discord and anger and criticism and confusion, you will no longer see so much anger and criticism and confusion.

You are creating everything that you see and you are then judging it and criticizing it further, and you are now living in a giant soup of anger and criticism. Try this... try not watching your news for ten days. Do not read about the problems of the world or governments and do not focus on problems. See only solutions if you do hear others speaking about the news. Know that the best or highest outcome will occur for any problem you may hear about, but do not intentionally watch or listen to your news. Your news has a job to do. Their job, like yours, is to make money and prosper. Well, they do their job well and they make money and profits by keeping you tuned in. The more people they attract, the bigger their audience grows. The bigger their audience, the better their ratings.

"You" are driving the direction of your news by what you are most curious about. And what are you most curious about? You are magnetic in nature and so you are drawn to what is in you. Your news reflects what its audience most wants to see because without an audience they must change their programming. You are basically programming your news by saying "This is what I like to see. This is what makes me tune in." Do you see too much violence on TV and in your movies? Guess what sells? You are literally asking the powers that be to create more of what you focus on. In the same way that you blow up your personal reality bubble by blowing your energy into it, you are blowing up your news reports and making them bigger and more valuable to you.

You create everything that you see to various degrees. If you do not watch your news for ten days you may feel a little lost from the lack of negativity coming into your mind. You feed you constant drama to keep you on your toes and ready for anything. It is not necessary to stress yourself in this way. As we discussed earlier, stress hormones are created in the body when you hear bad news, and these may block your immune system from performing as well as it could. You will find that joy and peaceful thoughts have a positive effect on your body and on your immune system. You can actually raise, or boost, your immune system by being happy.

So, for ten days feed your mind joy and happiness, and this will allow some of your anger and upset to leave you. Any upset that you carry is a direct result of anger or sorrow. Either of these will bring you down and, in this class, we are now learning to rise "up" to love and light. You will do well with this. Use your curiosity to see how well you do on this little diet away from negativity. You may find that you are hooked on news and drama. Do not worry if you are. You will rise up eventually, simply because you are a loving light being who is just being held down artificially until you can learn to release your anchor and sail away. You will get there eventually, so do not add greater stress or worry if you are not ready to haul anchor now. You are loved just as you are, and remember – this is just a game that you souls like to play.

≈∭≈

*Y*ou will find that you are most agreeable when you are happy. Happiness is a state of mind. Happiness is determined by your mind when you choose it. You may choose to be happy when you wish to, by letting go of the feelings that you are focusing on that are blocking happiness.

Say you have a headache and you are upset because you want to feel good. Try this... the next time you have an ache or a pain, decide that it is simply a physical problem that is leaving you. You feel it because it is rising up and leaving. Your headache is actually criticism that is leaving you. And since all criticism is self-criticism, you are releasing your self-criticism and judgments. Make this a good thing and celebrate the fact that this energy is leaving you. If you are good at visualization, you may send hearts and flowers and balloons and even confetti to your head. This will lighten the intensity of your pain because you will be sending light, fun and happy energy, in these forms, to your mind and brain. The brain will translate this into a good event and your energy will shift in that direction.

It is always possible to work with your body when it is trying to release energy. Usually, your body will use pain as a signal to let you know that there is too much energy buildup in one area. This is how you know to get off your feet when you twist an ankle or break a leg. Body is always trying to communicate with you, but you are often too busy with life to listen... it is often told to shut up by taking a pain pill. So now your body feels the need to scream louder to get you to listen and so you take more, or stronger, pills. The best way to deal with body is, first off, to apologize for ignoring it and filling it with dense, heavy energy. Then you may begin to communicate and to nurture your body as though it were a living entity; for it is a living, breathing entity that carries you where you want to go. You must learn to love and accept your beautiful body just as it is. It does you no good to insult your body or to criticize it in any way.

Love you – body, mind and soul. You are beautiful and magnificent and quite miraculous and you are ignorant of this fact. You are the most beautiful of your creations and you have forgotten how you created all of this for your own pleasure. It is as though you turned from being a talented creator into a very harsh judge. Let your body be. Stop judging yourself so harshly. Love you! Nurture you. Talk to yourself and tell yourself how much you love and appreciate you and your life on earth. Look in your mirror every day and say, "I love you! I really, really love you!"

You are only what you choose to believe that you are. It's time now to come over to love and release all those judgments that you have been pounding you down with. Let it all come to the surface and leave you. Let go of your troubles and worries and fears and criticism. Let it all go and switch over to trust and acceptance that everything is okay, until you can move into acceptance that everything is good. You will switch over to a new track of thinking and this will allow you to heal. Be patient with this healing process and do not give up on you and your creative abilities.

❧

For the most part you do not believe that you create what you see. You are programmed to believe that life is what happens to you and you do not see how you may be interacting with life and causing some instances to occur.

You have been in the dark as to where you come from and who you are. You do not feel like you are from a light being and part of a light being. I wish I could show you how beautiful and wonderful you truly are. You do not come here because it is hard to be human, you actually come here because you want to experience emotions and feelings and sensations. You want this when you are back home in the light. You have no way of seeing life on earth when you are not in a body of some sort. You do not feel sad or lonely when you are not in a body of some sort. You do not feel accomplishment and that rush you get from winning when you are not in a body of some sort. You do not feel the joy of dancing without a body and you do not feel the comfort of a hug.

You come here to earth because you can and because it is a great ride. It is fun and it can be challenging, and you love it. You are simply using a body to express in another dimension. You are not here to be miserable; you are here to enjoy this ride… this game that you play with yourself and with your soul friends. Please do not take it so seriously. It is not meant to be hell, it is meant to be fun and maybe even heaven. You have decided that it is dangerous to be human and that idea takes all the fun and entertainment out of your game.

Please come back to love and acceptance. Please let go of your fears and your criticisms of how things should be and begin to accept things as they are. You became a little too harsh with your judgments and it's time now to calm down and begin to see what you are creating. When you are constantly judging and hostile, you only draw more of the same to you. Move over to calm and peaceful thoughts and guess what you will "receive?" It's time now to let go of your outrage about how wrong things are and let go of your defense and attack mode. Let everything be what it is and allow yourself to breathe. You are afraid, and your body is tied up in knots simply because you are exhausting yourself with all the fear that you are running through the cells of your body.

Breathe… just breathe… that is the only thing you really need to do. Let go of everything else and simply "be." You have forgotten how to just be alive and happy because you have become so goal oriented, and so afraid of not having, that you are pushing at you constantly. You have become overly concerned with making a good life for yourself, and you will feel better when you come into balance and appreciate who you are right now. It is one thing to dream and open up to your dreams and is quite another to push yourself forward out of fear and terror of the unknown. When you have high hopes and wishes, you move forward more easily. When you are pushing at yourself to achieve, you may feel put upon and begin to resent your own self. You may not like yourself and this will cause you to dislike others. You cannot love them if you cannot love you.

So, let go of your need to push you around and begin to love and accept you just as you are. You came here because it's fun. Let it be fun and games. Don't be so afraid of life and death on earth. It's not real! You are acting out a role in a play. Change your play from drama to comedy or even romance. Get off the drama train and ride the happiness train. Less seriousness – more fun.

Now, when you are sick or injured, I do not expect you to be happy about it, but you may still laugh and joke about it and this will assist your body in feeling better and possibly in healing faster. You have all seen or heard of people who have great illness and have a remarkable attitude in the midst of suffering. This is the most helpful response to any illness or disease. Illness is often just a symptom of something that is out of balance in the body or mind, and this approach can be most helpful in bringing things back into balance. There is such a thing as spontaneous remission and this is common among you.

When you learn to not take everything so seriously and when you calm down and let yourself be exactly where you are, you will be accepting you just as you are and will no longer be pushing you around and trying to control everything out of your fear of what may occur. You are learning here to love and accept you just as you are, and you are letting go of your fear that you have done something wrong. Some of you believe that there is something basically wrong with you personally. There is not. You are perfect just the way you are and you only require a little love and acceptance. Love and acceptance is the best medicine, and love and acceptance will heal you. Run the energy of acceptance through your body day and night and you will feel so much better. Accept you, accept life on earth, and accept that you are part of God!

꾊

*Y*ou have a wonderful way of acknowledging your belief in wrong and right. You believe strongly that wrongdoing must be punished in some way and that right doers must be rewarded in some way. This leads you to believe that if you do something wrong, you will be caught and punished and if you are not caught, you spend your time in fear of when you might be caught.

You have spent a great deal of time waiting for the other shoe to drop or waiting for life to punish you for your sins. This causes you to live in constant fear and you do so unconsciously. Once you let go of this belief in right and wrong, you will be giving yourself a great big gift. You will be letting go of a huge weight inside of you. This is why I council you to let go of judgment. Your belief in right and wrong behavior has created some of your biggest barriers to rising up to the higher dimensions.

You have come into a world that is based on duality, however, you may choose to break free and rise above to the dimensions of wholeness and awareness. This is done by simply letting go of all that you now hold on to as your moral code. This will be quite difficult for any of you who use your moral code to rise above others and also use it to be smarter and closer to God. You honestly believe in a punishing God and so you are trying to save yourself from the punishment of hell. The big news here is that there is no such place as hell or Hades. It's all made up and God, your Source, never ever sends anyone anywhere as a punishment. You must begin to believe in an all accepting, all loving God for your own sake. If you continue to believe in a punishing God, you will continue to live in fear of death and in fear of life. This is due to the fact that you will continue to believe that God is out to get you or even that life is out to get you. This is no way to live, and I will tell you now that this type of belief will bring you down when your true wish is to go "up."

You will find that the more you let go of your belief in right and wrong, the better you will feel. You will begin to see how everything here on earth has been made up in an attempt to survive and in an attempt to figure out what is going on and why things often go in a downward direction. You are often confused because you do not see how energy works and how you may assist by raising yourselves up to a higher level of vibration. You only move up or down according to thoughts and feelings. You do not go up or down by staying in a comatose state and not thinking or feeling. You are energy in motion and therefore, you are always moving and changing.

So; you might move and change to a more positive view of God and this will allow you to rise a little higher vibration wise. Why? Well, for one thing, you are God, so it might be a good idea to stop judging God as an ogre who punishes those who do the least little thing wrong, when there is no wrong in God's perspective. So, let it go! You do not want, nor do you need, to carry around this subconscious fear that you must one day face your maker who will then judge you. This is nonsense and it is superstition.

You will find that the easiest way to stop putting judgment in your body to bring you down is to let go of any belief in wrong. This allows you to let go of its opposite which is right. Right behavior will no longer exist and you will no longer be using this duality to enforce your rules on yourself. When you let go of right behavior, you will no longer be so confused and wonder which direction is right for you, or which mate is right for you, or which job is right to you. You will begin to accept what is offered if it feels good, and you will let go of anything that does not feel good. This may sound like duality to you since I am using the word good, however, I can only speak to you in language that you will relate to and understand. I have chosen to communicate with you through a woman who is not considered well educated, and this allows me to speak in simple clear language that is easily understood by most.

So, you will arrive at a place where you only use your feelings to determine your choices. You will no longer confuse yourself with all the details involved in your choices. One way will simply feel good or easier or more comfortable to you. You seem to have an issue with comfort at times and this too is programming. A good fit is always more comfortable than forcing yourself to do something that does not fit. It is always okay to be you and to accept you just as you are. You often spend your time reaching for the gold ring when you could easily sit and wait for God (you) to deliver your good to you.

So – I told you at the beginning of this writing that you have a wonderful way of creating duality and that is because you have a wonderful way of creating, no matter what you happen to be creating. It is all good. You are all good!

ℂℂ

*Y*ou will find that you love to be part of the crowd. You do not want to stray too far from what others are doing and you most certainly do not wish to move into unacceptable behavior. You hate being left out and left behind. Well, now is a good time to be different and to follow your own path. This may cause you problems, and also you may find moving in a new direction to be so unfamiliar as to cause you to feel confused. After all, you will be moving into the unknown.

You all fear what you do not understand and you all like to follow a known path. This allows you to hold on to your current ways and your current attitudes and even your current habits. For the most part, you are a creature of habit and this has caused you to stay in a rut or to repeat problem-causing behavior. You are well aware of society's fight against drug and alcohol use, and most of you agree with efforts to stop the abuse of such chemicals and stimulants. You however, do not agree with the use of mind control and some of you even disagree with spirit communication. You have a great deal of fear concerning your own thoughts and feelings. You have never quite accepted the emotional body, and the mental body frightens you. You all fear any type of mention regarding mental problems.

Well, once again I will tell you to love and accept all parts of you. Try not to fear your emotions and try not to fear your thoughts. It's all energy moving within you and this energy is often trying to come up and out of you. You may have suppressed memories that are now healing and wanting to leave you. You may also have emotional trauma from the past that is now trying to leave you. After all, this is a time of healing anything and everything that is not of love. So I would suggest to you that you allow for unusual feelings and thoughts at this time. Do not fear your thoughts and do not fear your feelings. Allow all energy to pass through you and to rise to the surface. Know that you are healing and know that healing includes change.

You do not like change and you do not like to feel unsettled. So if you have unsettling feelings in you from past judgment, how are you going to get those energies up and out of you if you will not free them to rise to the surface? Whenever you have uncomfortable thoughts, you may simply allow them to be okay by realizing that they are simply leaving you and allowing you to lighten your load. Often you find yourself on a spiritual path and then you incur a bump in the road, so you decide your path may not be such a good idea.

Stay centered by allowing for circumstances to occur that you may not understand. No one taught you to be a spirit being. No one told you in childhood how you are a spiritual being simply having a human experience. You will do well to teach yourself that all is really okay and that you are energy moving within, and interacting with, energy. You are doing so well when you reach the level where you are actually clearing and releasing the denser energies of fear and confusion. Do not be afraid when you see others who are releasing their fear and confusion. You are not the only one who is healing. Light is entering this dimension and as light enters, shifts occur. This is a time of great healing and, if you are energy, you will be affected in some way.

So please be gentle and kind with yourself and with those among you who do not understand what they are experiencing. Most humans who are clearing fear will also clear the anger and rage that is attached to the fear. This is a time of healing and not everyone will understand how things are actually getting better and not getting worse. Luckily you are reading the kind of information that allows you to see from a different perspective. Do not judge those who do not see as you see. Allow everyone to walk their own path and to be guided by their own spirit or soul. You are not in charge of them and you are barely in charge of you. Let it go. Let everything be what it is until "you" can rise to a perspective that is high enough to see what is really going on.

For the most part, you do not accept yourself as good. You all feel that you are not good enough and this causes you to fear one another. Because you harshly judge your own behavior, you often believe that others are seeing your flaws and seeing you as you see you. You are afraid of not being wanted and not being accepted. This is due, in part, that you do not accept various traits which are part of your personality and your makeup.

You are mostly judging you based on your programming and on your belief in good vs. bad and wrong vs. right. It will be difficult for you to let go of these beliefs and patterns if you have held tightly to your identity of being morally right and a good saintly person. The more it is important to you to be seen as good and righteous, the harder it may be to simply accept that you are inherently love and goodness. You will find that you need to project an image of goodness in order to feel safe.

Now – this is not to infer that there are not good people walking the earth. It is only to let you know that you may be one of those who do not believe you are inherently good, and so you cover up your dislike of your own self by acting perfect and, what you believe to be, good. Perfectionists are mostly trying to please in order to be accepted by others. When you care so much about what others think and how others perceive you, you are often trying to protect yourself from harm. This means you find others to be dangerous and you fear them.

Fear comes in many forms and is often tied into your personal daily lives in many ways. Once you move over to self-love, you will find it much easier to be yourself. It's a good idea to be around situations and groups where you feel safe and accepted, as it will allow your nervous system to calm down and it will allow you to know what it feels like to be accepted, which will assist you in accepting your own self. Often people who do not feel good about themselves will project that persona onto others. When a human is feeling bad, they often project their negative feelings forward onto others. This is a way of gaining a group mentality and being accepted as a victim. Often those who feel bad actually feel down emotionally and they may feel comforted if others go down emotionally also. You need not follow the crowd and you need not hate and despise what others hate and despise. It is okay to break away from negative beliefs and begin to accept life as it is. It is okay to be different and to move up even when others wish you to stay down with them. It is okay to break away from the pack and the strong pull of duality.

When you first begin to "accept" life and "accept" yourself just as you are, you will be turning away from years and years of programming. You may feel like you do not fit in anywhere and this will be a direct result of breaking away from duality. You will feel the pull of energy to return, however, if your spirit guidance is strong enough you will be able to rise above duality with a certain amount of ease. Do not be concerned when you have moments where you stumble backwards. This is a "process" of rising up; this is not an instantaneous, overnight event. You are slowly and gradually being lifted up and this causes you to pull "up" all your various anchors (beliefs) that have assisted in holding you down.

You will find that the greater your fear of others and how they see you or accept you, the more difficult it may be for you to leave duality behind. It does not matter... it only matters that you "desire" to rise in awareness and your desire will ultimately get you there. So, do not be concerned about action or inaction right now. Simply enjoy the ride and know that you are moving on "up."

You will find that you cannot talk others into going with you; however, your energy affects everyone else and everything else on this planet. You will do well with this process of ascension and you will see the results in due time.

I love you and I welcome you to the world of spirit, better known as heaven. It takes time but you are well on your way!

৯৬

*Y*ou have always wanted more. You love to gain and, of course, you hate to lose. This makes it difficult for you to let go and flow with life. You fear letting go, as you feel that you might end up in a bad place. You will do well to remember that you are always guided and you always contain soul/spirit energy. You have all that you require right inside of you. You are the divine that you pray to and you "are" the love that you so desire.

Once you begin to take in and receive more and more positive thought energy, you will begin to notice a shift in your thinking. Instead of focusing on all the negative situations and possible outcomes, you will be focusing on positive situations and outcomes. This will literally "move you" in a more positive direction and you will attract more positive energy to you. Remember you are a giant magnet and you just happen to draw to you more of what you are. So, in times of clearing and releasing dense energy you may possibly draw more dense energy to you. This cannot be avoided since you are this giant magnet; however, once you have released and cleared your negative energy, it will leave you and you will then be lighter and you will be carrying less dense energy due to the clearing.

So; do not be concerned when you feel like you are going backward, you are not! You are healing, and because you are healing and letting go of your hold on dense energy, you are able to rise up a little higher and your perspective may then shift up to the next level. Once you have shifted "up" even a tiny bit, you begin to receive energy from your new higher vibration. Basically, anytime you let go of dense thoughts and beliefs, you allow yourself to rise just that much. You are literally energy, and the universe is energy, and God is energy. You are always responding to energy and energy response to you. Do not be concerned when you feel overwhelmed by energy. It is always moving and shifting and changing. You are energy and so you are always moving and shifting and changing.

You will gradually get to a level in your rise up where there will be no effort to heal. You will automatically be more positive than negative, and this will allow you to rise above the fray and to stay at this higher perspective. You will automatically feel a sense of well being and you will just "know" that all is well. This is when you will begin to experience life on earth as more like heaven on earth. You may achieve this level and be very happy with yourself and with life in general. This is quite doable for you and you will most enjoy your creation of heaven on earth. You may experience wonderful synchronicities and you may feel like your life has become quite magical. This will be a wonderful time for you and you will most enjoy the ride.

You will find that life will give you your desires and you will become aware of how you create. You will automatically turn away from any negative programming in an effort to stay "high." You will most enjoy this type of freedom from fear and you will thrive. Do not give up on you and do not give up on love (acceptance). You are well on your way now. You have the tools you require, the information you have been reading will guide you up to the next level. Stay positive, love yourself, look to your soul for guidance and you will do very well on your rise up to the next level.

You are God energy expressing through a human body. Let yourself be aware that you are perfect just the way you are. Let yourself know that all is well and you are safe no matter what is going on around you. Let yourself know that you are loved and accepted by loving and accepting you. Let yourself know that you are ready and you are quite capable of letting go of fear. You will do well with this. The more you remind yourself of these truths the easier it is to move away from the lies. This is what all the talk regarding "removing the veil of untruth" is about. It's not about catching everyone in their lies to you. It is about catching "you" in your lies to you. You are divine and you are innocent of all charges you may have leveled against you.

You are at your turning point now. You may continue to lie to yourself about who and what you are or you may tell yourself the truth. Do not follow any teaching that leads you to believe that you are "less than." You are actually more than you will realize for some time to come. Stay true to yourself and know that you are not only part of God; you also carry God within you. You are made of God energy and that energy is creative in nature. Creative energy has the ability to shift and change into whatever it is pushed into. You have been sending you in a specific direction by your thoughts and beliefs. Change your thoughts and your beliefs and you will move in a new direction.

It is just that easy, love you and accept you, and you will be loving and accepting all that is. You are the director and the producer of your life. You may create the most beautiful life movie simply by changing your mind!

You will find that you most easily connect with those who support you and lift you up in emotional ways. Those who lift you up are probably those who you seek out. You are all connected so it is easy to see how you affect one another. As you seek those who lift you up be sure to watch how you respond. Those who lift you up do not judge you and they do not judge others. Those who lift you higher do not condemn any other group or any other individual. Those who lift you up are focused on the positive in everyone, not just the positive in a few. Those who lift you up will leave you feeling safe and not feeling in danger from others. Those who lift you up will have the ability to show you how you are going to be okay no matter what occurs.

I hope you realize how your belief system can bring you up or down and how your belief system can restore you or tear you down. When you find yourself listening to those who are tearing down others, I hope you will remember to not focus on such beliefs. It is okay to have preferences and it is okay to admire and respect certain traits, however, when you put others down, you put you down. This is the basic thing to remember about being an energy being. You are literally connected energetically to everyone else, and where you try to send them, you are actually sending you.

So, for many of you this will be a good guide on how well you are doing in creating well-being for yourself. Good positive thoughts 'in' equal good positive energy 'in'. You need not worry and you need not focus on scary negative results. You may focus on good, positive results and this will eventually allow you to live in good positive results. You may use this creative process in any area of your life and it will assist you in many, many ways.

This is a good time to remind you that you are always loved and always assisted and guided. You are never alone and you are watched over and accepted by many in the spirit world. You have no idea how vast you are and how many parts of you there may be. You are a multi-dimensional being of light and love. You inhabit a body in order to experience this material world. You may raise your level of awareness while still in a body. You need not die to see how you are spiritual. You may return to the awareness that you are a light being simply by reminding yourself that you are. You may reconnect with your soul simply by reminding yourself that you are soul and you contain soul.

You are not here to be alone, you are here to wake up and rise up to the awareness that you created the material world of illusion and then you dove into it. You live in an energetic dream. You are walking around in an illusion. Make the best of it by seeing the best in it. You control how you see everything. Do not bring you down by wishing you could bring them down. Why do you think that Jesus and other great teachers taught to love your neighbor as yourself? Why do you think that the one thing taught in most belief systems is to rise above negativity? It's all here for you to learn. You are literally teaching yourself to go higher in awareness. This allows you to vibrate faster, which allows you to thrive.

The cells and atoms that make up your body are loaded with information in the form of energy. You have libraries of information stored in you. You may remember some, but most is far removed from you and is only affecting you subconsciously. You are vast indeed. You are multi-dimensional and you exist everywhere... even in that person you are judging and wanting to put down. End war now... it is a waste of time and energy. No one ever dies and hatred does not serve you well. If you really want to rise up I hope you realize how "you" control it all!

⚘

You have always been afraid of something. It is built into your nervous system and is part of you. You are fearful out of a need to protect yourself, do not judge this part of you. You are learning, or becoming aware, of all parts of you. You are simply waking up to who you are and how you operate. This is nothing new, however you are just now becoming aware of all that you contain.

You do not require change if you do not wish to change. You may continue on as you always have and you will be just fine. You will always, always, always be accepted and loved by God and by many others who watch over you. You are never alone, you never take a wrong turn and you are always accepted just as you are. The purpose of this book and the information given here is to lighten your load and make life a little more pleasant for you. If you continue to see life as you always have, it will not create any difference in how you now live. If, however, you wish to create a difference in how you perceive and receive life, this information will be most helpful to you.

So; you need not change unless you wish to change and you need not judge yourself in any way whatsoever. You are creative energy enjoying the benefits of your creativity. You are playing in an energy playground of your own making and everything is good and well. You are expressing and loving and acting out a role – no big trauma if you do not wish to change how you play this role. Please do not put pressure on yourself to change or to be different. This is about "flowing" with

145

energy, it is not about fighting energy and bending energy to your will. Acceptance is key here.

So, wherever you are, what ever you are doing, "accept you." Love you and nurture you and be very thankful to be you. You are an incredible soul who is playing in a very dense dimension. Support you by supporting your choices. Know that when you make a choice to go in one direction or another it is for a good reason. You often don't know why you move one way or another, but know that everything you do is for a reason you may not be aware of.

When it comes to love and acceptance you will receive what is best for your purposes at that particular time. Some of you have made agreements that allow you to experience certain levels of energy that will assist in pushing you in specific directions. This is usually done in an effort to experience specific lessons or to grow in specific areas. Most agreements are changeable once you decide to change them. Life agreements such as staying with the same soul friend for a lifetime or having a certain soul friend come in as your child are all changeable. You are not locked into any agreement you have made before or after entering this lifetime. You are flexible and changeable and your life is flexible and changeable.

Once you figure out what you want and what your next move is, you will wish to continue to love and accept yourself. If you take away only one thing from this entire book, I hope that will be to love and accept "all" that you are. This is the greatest gift that you can give to you. Love you and accept you no matter how angry or sad or frustrated or ugly that you feel. Always know that you are the light of love trying to express in various ways through matter. Just the fact that you made it into the material plane is a miracle. You are light energy expressing in a dark energy environment. You were clever enough to make it into this dimension and now you can assist yourself by raising 'all' up into awareness.

You've got this! You will do very well with this part you are playing. You are the star of this show! It's your turn to shine and you are doing really, really well....

❧

$\mathcal{I}$t is always possible to be who you wish to be. It is always possible to find what you wish to find and it is always possible to draw to you that which you wish to experience. Be brave and walk into your future knowing that energy is what you are and energy is what you draw to you. Once you begin to see everything as energy, you will begin to realize how all movement in this dimension occurs.

Know that when you truly desire peace, you will begin to emit peaceful thoughts and peaceful ideas. Peace is a state of mind and peace begins with you. You literally live within your own personal reality, and you may fill your personal reality with peace no matter what is occurring around you. If you happen to live in a war zone, you may find it difficult to have peace of mind. The best way to deal with war is to always know that it will end and that you will be taken care of in some way. You need not fear war and you need not draw war to you personally. You may avoid war and conflict by hiding from it within your own psyche. You have this wonderful ability to pretend and to make-believe. It is okay to pretend that certain things do not exist for you, and this has assisted many in times of chaos.

You are an imaginative being who has the ability to create. You may rise above any situation simply by seeing it differently and often by pretending it is something else. You may pretend that any hurtful situation is actually a game where you must find your way to safety. This is common among your young who survive adult situations at a very early age. You will find that pretending is simply a way of creating and it allows you to keep your nervous system in order and it allows you to make it through many difficult situations.

When you pretend your way out of something that is traumatic, you may end up dealing with your emotional trauma after the event is over and played out. You all try to face situations and not pretend that everything is okay, however, there are times when pretending is your answer to saving your mind and subsequent peace of mind. This is not an easy topic to discuss with you and Liane is having trouble writing this for me. However, I have control over her arm and hand and she allows me to write what I feel is necessary to heal you.

When you land in a war zone through no fault of your own, I will remind you that on a soul level you come into this dimension with a blueprint for your life. Often you wish to experience specific events and situations. Even war is considered when entering this world of illusion. It's often referred to as one of the big lessons to experience. Of course, when you are soul energy you know you do not die, so it's pretty much all fun and games like in your childhood games where you just pretend to die. This is what you are doing when you play your war games. You may even be choosing sides before you enter earth. Your soul knows that it never ever ends and it knows that you never ever end. You are taken to the next level of awareness when you die or cross over in this life. It is beautiful and it feels very, very freeing and good.

You will find that the scariest part of death is your "fear." Whatever you fear about death is always what drives your thoughts and beliefs regarding death. Let it go! You are creating a terrible feeling about something that need not be

148

terrible. I realize that this is upsetting for you to read, however, it is time for you to realize how you truly do create how you "view" everything. You need not make life a villain and you need not make death a villain. There are many, many aspects to you that you are completely unaware of. Let your fear of death go and replace it with acceptance and love. Always know that when you leave the illusion, you wake up as your true self. You see that you are God force and that you are back in your Source.

It is like waking up from a dream and you end up back in your true reality. Do not fear the life you live, it's just your game, your play, your fun. Do not fear leaving the game you are playing for you will be safe and loved and back to your true self as a spirit being minus the material world. You simply take off your costume and you return home.

Now; the reason I am writing this to you and, in the process, possibly making you very uncomfortable is simply because you fear death so much that it causes problems for you. You literally make yourself sick when you take in too much fear and I am assisting in your healing. You heal by letting go of everything that is causing you discomfort. This is one of the biggest fears that is most draining for you. You may let go of fear by holding in mind how you are not really here and you are simply dreaming. When you die you go within to your true identity and you become conscious. Right now you are walking around in an unconscious state....

༄༅

Before you know it you will be on your way to happiness and joy of life. You will let go of most concerns and you will flow with the energy of life. This will be due to the fact that you see things differently. The purpose of getting you to see things differently is to point you in a new direction. Living in fear and concern and worry really brings you down and I want to assist in lifting you up. If you can just see all as it truly is, you will no longer be living in fear; you will have moved over into trust. Trust will set you free and trust will allow you to flow.

So; no matter what is occurring around you simply trust that all will turn out well. If you cannot see it as turning out well, simply tell yourself that it will be okay. Okay is much higher in vibration and okay will draw okay energy to it. The entire purpose of getting you to see how things really are is to help you. You want help and you constantly request helpful answers to your many questions. Some of you pray for help by focusing on what you don't want, and I would like you to realize how this may not be helpful to you. It is always, always best to remind yourself to focus on what you do want and your thoughts will be going in an upward direction.

I have written a series of books through Liane which are most helpful in turning you inward to your own God self. For those of you who feel the need for more information on healing, I highly recommend this series of twenty books. You may find more answers to guide you in your awakening process. (You will find a list of titles in the back of this book)

You need not concern yourself with what others are doing, for you live "in" you and you are receiving guidance for you personally. If you are reading this book you have somehow been guided by your soul to receive, or at least read, this information. It does not matter if this book was a gift, as it is you who decided to pick it up and read it. Your soul will send you helpful information for your specific path and your soul friends will be guiding their humans in the same way. Some will be guided to different beliefs and different countries and different religions. Each soul has a purpose and each has a part to play. No two souls will *incringe on the path of another. In the spirit world diversity is well known and respected. It is the same in any play or movie – you do not act out someone else's role, you act out your role. You do not mess up the play by telling everyone else to act the part that you personally are playing.

I don't care if it is your child or your mate, or your parent – live and let live! Allow everyone to be exactly who they are. They have guidance just as you do and the greatest gift you can give is love and acceptance. Do not go into extreme thinking here. I am not asking you to allow your loved one to become an ax murderer. Let's keep things in balance and always stay in your center. For those of you who work in psychiatry, you have been sought out and requested to help, or offer guidance, and this is for a reason. Do not become overbearing and always respect boundaries.

You have all learned a great deal in your lifetime and there is always more to learn. For now it is best to assimilate all that you have learned and to remember how you are a soul, a light energy, moving and living in and expressing through a human form. You are a beautiful example of creation and you are so much greater than you have been taught. What you have been taught so far has gotten you this far, so do not judge anything that you have ever experienced. There is absolutely a reason for everything, and you are working and living in the dark as to what is really going on.

You will continue to learn and to grow in the direction of your choice. Your world of illusion will not end, however, it is transforming and it is growing into a paradise for you. You will create your heaven on earth by focusing on heaven on earth. Know that you are currently in a construction site that is being transformed into something new and beautiful. You are changing, and as "you" change, all that you see and how you see it changes. This is a most magical and productive time! It is wonderful and soon you will see the wonder of it all.

Do not give up on feeling positive. Do not fear change and construction work. Do not fear being left behind. Your desire to rise higher will automatically lift you higher. Do not fear the denser energies as they are vibrated loose from within your cells. Do not fear healing and clearing and releasing. And please, let go of your fear of God.

*Note: I'm not familiar with the word "incringe" so I did some research. Here's what I found: "Incringe" is a word that is occasionally used to combine the words "infringe" and "encroach." It is used more frequently in spoken English than in print.

Liane

❧

Before you know it you will return to a state of grace. Grace is when you realize how you are good and innocent. Grace is when you know that all is good and innocent. It will be so simple for you to forgive and for you to understand how nothing is wrong and everything is simply energy in movement. Living on earth will no longer feel like a struggle simply because you will have released your fear regarding life. You will let go of fear and move into trust. You will "know" in a very sure and certain way that you are not alone and you are always taken care of.

If war comes you will be safe and if a storm comes, you will be safe. Safety comes when you let go of your strong belief in danger. Do not forget how you are magnetic in nature and you draw like energy to you. You need not fear life and you need not fear death. You choose to come to experience the illusion of both. Do not fear this game that you play. Rise above this game to the next dimension. Raise your thoughts and your beliefs and your desires up to the next level. This will raise you up to another level where fear is less powerful. The more fear you release, the higher you go. Do not judge yourself for releasing your fears and do not judge others for releasing their fear energy.

Know that all is occurring as it is meant to occur. Know that all are seeing what they are meant to see, and know that all will be perceived as it is meant to be perceived by each individual. You do not control their reality and you only slightly control your own.

So, as you go along I wish you to stay as high in your thinking as possible. I wish you to know peace by turning away from war and chaos. I wish you to continue to see all through the eyes of love, and I wish you to continue to love, accept and approve of yourself. Know that you are God expressing through matter in a fun game called "Change from spirit to human and back again." You are doing a great job here on earth and you are moving in the direction you planned to take. Now it is only a matter of time until you discover your true self and learn to exist as a spiritual being.

This is a most magnificent time. The people of earth are healing and releasing trapped energy and all is going well. Enlightenment is simply a matter of releasing enough dark energy that you may lighten up a bit. Life on earth is not meant to be so serious and scary; life on earth is meant to be fun. Love you and love all that you see. If you see something you do not like, you are simply looking in the wrong place. Look again in a new direction. Change "your" personal view of life on earth and you will tune into a new earth. This is not a stagnant universe. Everything here is moving and changing according to how you move it and change it.

You are the catalyst! You are God creating through matter. God trumps matter. God moves matter. God is cause and God creates. You are God in a body. You are a part of God expressing through a person. Be all that you can be. Trust that all is well and let go of creating preconceived thoughts of danger. In your efforts to protect yourself, you are projecting fear out into the future. It is not enough that you fear the present, now you are sending your fears into your future. Please stay in the now. Stop projecting into your future until you can learn to project love, acceptance and compassion for all that exists here.

You are spreading fear energy into all possible realities when you project such theories and beliefs. Stay where you are now. Sit down and think peace... feel peace and know peace.

⚜

For the most part you are a lovely version of spirit. You walk and talk and move with grace. You do understand a great deal and you do believe the best is yet to come.

You have found yourselves in a position of not knowing if life is as good as it could be. Life as you now see it is mostly a mystery to you. You may find your answers and you may discover your truth by going within. It really is true that everything that you require is right inside of you. Most of what you now know has been programmed into you, and you only require letting go of all that programming in order to remove your blocks to your own divinity. You are truly a divine being and your only problem, or block to seeing your divinity, are all those teachings that convinced you that you are not divine.

So, my job, and the purpose of all that I write through Liane, is to show you the way home. This project was agreed upon by many, as a way of showing those who stumble across the information a way back home to love. Nothing is really necessary except the desire to rise up. Nothing is required except acceptance, which is allowing and then embracing all that is. Once you realize how everything has a purpose, you will let go of your need to push everything into a category of good or bad, right or wrong. You will begin to allow life to unfold and you will no longer give your power away to fear. Fear will only bring you deeper into fear, and after fear comes paranoia. Please let go of your dance with fear. Please stop entertaining fear.

Once you let go of fear, you will easily embrace love of all. It is most difficult for you to feel love when you are in the midst of judging someone or something as not good. You will find that the easiest way to get aboard the love train is to ignore those things you hate. This will allow you to come into balance; and from balance (or your center) it is only a hop, skip and a jump into love. Move to the love side of you. Love will envelop you and love will take you over. It is like going to a beautiful spa for a week. You totally disconnect with stress and your fears; and you focus on health and nature and peace and calm. Do that! Be in a state of total peace... maybe you can do this one day a week. Then, after you get the hang of it, you can think and feel calm and peace for a second day during your week.

You may use this technique until you have found your center. Once you move to your center, the pull of fear will not be so strong on you, and you will find it easier and easier to stay centered and out of chaos and stress and strain. Do yourself a favor by giving your psyche and your mind a break from all those stress hormones that dilute your healing powers. You will find that your healing ability rises when you rise. Your healing ability is directly related to stress and this is why heart problems are on the rise. You may literally heal you by showing love and feeling love... not romantic love, although that is affective also, but compassion and acceptance are a good choice of medicine.

Feed you love and acceptance. Allow "you" to enjoy the gift of acceptance. Allow you to know how good you are and how divine you are. You are not a sinner, you are not a nobody and you are not bad. You are a divine expression of God. You are all that is positive and beautiful if you will only "allow" that part of you to shine through. You are simply afraid to let the real you shine through. After all, you have been very strongly programmed to believe how you are wrong, and you were told "No – you're doing it wrong" all those times in your formative years. You are not wrong, you are an evolving, growing entity and you are highly underrated right now.

Rate yourself higher! See yourself as powerfully divine. See your soul in you. Love your soul in you. Accept your soul in you. You walk around and judge you when it is not necessary. You are a walking, talking, breathing soul. You are a light being in a body! How much better can it get than that? You create, you have emotions, and you are God incarnate!

☙❧

From the time that you began to breathe, you have been trying to determine who you are and how you fit in. You are very confused by the time that you begin to talk, and you are extremely confused by the time that you become a teenager.

Your hormones tend to kick in around this time and you would normally begin to rebel. If, however, you were abused in your earlier years, you would more than likely be looking for a safe place to exist.

Those of you who were abused in childhood seek shelter and safety above all else. You may have a difficult time relating to your friends who were nurtured and lovingly cared for and this is natural. What I would like you to realize is how you may have planned your life path before you entered earth. Some of you have chosen soul friends to act out specific roles this lifetime, based on roles you may have played in previous lifetimes. This allows you, as spirits, to interact in the roles that you play. Usually, when working on a most difficult role, you request help from those souls you truly trust and even look up to for their ability to act out a role.

Do not worry if you have difficult people in your life, and try to understand how they may be a gift and a helper in reality. When you request a soul friend to play a role for you, it could be that you played that same role for them in a past life. This is not a karmic thing and it is not a tit for tat thing. This is soul kindness and souls understanding that you evolve and learn and grow as humans. This is how you grow. You do not learn a lot about being a human with feelings if you never experience your feelings. You don't learn much as a human if you never feel the joy of overcoming hatred and anger. You don't learn much about being a human with emotions if you never learn how to manage your emotions.

Once you learn how to rise above all emotional turmoil, you will feel so very happy. You will be at a whole new level of consciousness and you will feel confident in your choices. You will no longer struggle with the fear and confusion that you may have made the wrong choice. You will be clear! You will "know," without knowing how you know, which choice is best for where you now are. When you begin to trust yourself, you will be trusting your soul in its work and in its plan for you. Your soul is the part of you that remembers who you truly are. Your soul is you... the real you... the original you. You are soul incarnate. You are a living, breathing form of God and you are totally in the dark as to your true identity.

It is as though you have been judging yourself, and struggling, your entire life, and then you discover how you are really an extremely wealthy person of royalty. You are exulted and admired and revered and cared for. You are royalty and you have never been told how great and wonderful and magnificent that you are. You are like a diamond that has been laying in the mud. Now is the time to clean you off and spruce you up and allow you to shine. Do not be afraid that you are stupid and make wrong choices. Every choice may have been planned from the beginning by your aware, intelligent God-self or soul.

You are not stupid you are not wrong, you are simply unconscious as to who you truly are and who everyone else truly is. As you wake up, you will start with moments when you feel you are soul energy in a body. As you get closer to awareness, you will begin to "feel" how others are soul energy in a body also. You will no longer hold such harsh feelings towards others, as you will begin to see how and why they might be responding to life the way they are. As you see them for who they truly are, you will let go of your need to punish them. This is automatic once you begin to see them as a soul in a body. And, of course, you will continue to be aware that you too are God in a body.

You have so much to learn about who you are and who they truly are. Enjoy this ride you are on and continue to raise your thoughts to the higher possibilities. The higher you go in your thinking, the higher you take the rest of you. You are literally connected to everyone and everything. You are so grand and so great that you have lost track of parts of yourself.

In one of my earlier books, I explain how you are like a giant centipede that is so large that it circles the entire world and has come up on its own back end, but does not recognize its own back end. This centipede is so frightened by this giant back end that it bites his own butt. You are fighting "you" and you do not realize that you are all that is here....

❧

*Y*ou can always depend on your soul to guide you. Life may look like a maze to you; however, your soul has a higher perspective than you and may see obstacles that you do not foresee. You may end up moving in a strange (to you) direction, and it will turn out to be a big gift once you arrive at your destination. Do not discount your inner guidance and your intuition.

When you are born, you are taught to use your mind and to use your talents. No one teaches you to use your intuition. You are guided by the outside world to use good judgment and so judgment becomes very important to you. I would like you to rely on intuition in matters pertaining to future choices. Use your feelings more than your mind. Begin to trust your feelings and your intuition. Use your own guidance and rely on your soul to lead you out of any difficult choice you might incur.

You are a soul and once you begin to connect with and become friends with that part of you, you will be headed in a very good-for-you direction. Once you begin to work with and trust your soul, you will feel greater confidence in all your choices. You will begin to feel like all will go right, instead of feeling like everything always goes wrong. You will stop preparing yourself for the worst outcome and you will be allowing for the best outcome. It is all a matter of perspective, and because you are a creative force, you will be creating movement in the direction of your newly held perspective.

Perspective is everything and your personal perspective is very powerful in moving you in one direction or another. Always watch how you think and how you feel about things. Be aware of where you are coming from in your personal thought patterns, for where you are coming from determines where you go or move to. Be decisive in your choice to move higher and you will move higher. Make all choices and decisions from love and you will always go higher. There is no need to put yourself or anyone else down unless that is the direction you have decided to go. Words are not as important as the intention behind the words. You may tell someone they are being stupid in jest, but may really mean, "You are an idiot and I hate the way you act!" You may also tell someone that you love what an idiot they are and really mean, "You do the strangest things and I really like that about you!"

All is in the energy that is put into the words. Words of endearment are sometimes turned into weapons and manipulation. Be clear on your intention behind your words. Covert manipulation has become very popular and is not helpful to you if your goal is to rise higher. Manipulation has been used since time began and is a form of control due to fear of loss. You always want to control your environment in order to feel safe. Control gives you a false sense of security. You need not use control and subtle manipulation. You may rise above control to "trust." This will be a big change for all of you and you will find that fearful control is well ingrained in your behavior. I am asking you to let go and flow with life as much as you can. There is a great gift in simply letting go and floating.

You will find that trust and going with the flow will allow many, many gifts to flow your way. You may allow yourself to flow and you will be trusting you and your soul. You have basically been taught to not trust yourself or anyone else. Now I am asking you to trust and to allow your gifts to come to you.

❧

You have always existed as a being of light and you will always continue to exist as a being of light. You are never-ending and you will continue to be never-ending, so what are you afraid of? You go on forever and you play these wonderful games where you pretend to be human. You may play as long and as often as you wish. You may choose a long life or a short, brief life. It is all up to you and how you wish to create your life plan.

In reality, there is no death and nothing ever ends. You simply change to a new or different form. You do not go extinct and you do not wish to overstay your lifetime. You have many roles that you are currently playing in many other dimensions. You are the kings and queens of multitasking, and you are totally unaware that you exist in many dimensions at this time. You will become more aware of your interconnectedness and your expansiveness as you move to the higher dimensions of focus. You will learn how you exist in various levels and how you only focus on the level that you currently wish to view for whatever reasons.

You are simply not aware of this part of you. You "tune in" to that which you would like to view in the same way that you tune in to whichever channel you wish to view on your computer or television. You get to choose what you want to see. Choose your channel by wishing to view a particular reality.

You may live in fantasyland or you may tune into and live in mystery. You like drama? Okay – it's yours for the taking – simply "tune in." You do this on many levels and in many ways. Your thoughts are your remote control and will take you to the channel you wish to view. Once there, you may decide to view something else and this too is acceptable. It is all acceptable, and you may assist your experience of enjoyment by adjusting the channel for greater clarity.

Enjoy your viewing and enjoy this experience. If you are tired of living with the emotions that are being created in you by viewing this particular channel, simply use your thoughts to switch over to a different channel. Do you feel upset by what you are seeing? Simply see something different in its place. Pretend you are viewing hidden images within a picture. Look for the images that only make you feel good. Do not allow thoughts, that make you feel bad, creep in. Use your imagination to create a view (perspective) and a feeling that you like. Make it all up if you have to, until you get the hang of it and can turn all your moments into acceptable ones.

Once you have mastered the art of creating acceptable moments, it is just a short jump up to wonderful moments and loving gratitude. Your loving gratitude will lift you even higher and you will find yourself in unconditional love before you know it. This is where you thrive. This is where you excel, and this is where you meet your true soul self. You will find this a most enjoyable journey and it will become your life journey. You will be living a wonderful life of unconditional love with no judgment or condemnation. You will have risen above these denser energies and you will be creating all that you receive from this higher vibrating level. This enhances all that you draw to you to be of a higher vibration free of judgment and condemnation.

You will most enjoy this level and you will really enjoy the gifts that are magnetically drawn to you at this higher vibration. You are in control. Use your remote (thoughts) to tune in to that which you love and let go of all those other channels. You get to choose where you live by choosing what you view. You decide how your life will "feel" by choosing what you focus on. Your focus determines your happiness or unhappiness. Keep it light if you wish to be light in your feelings. Let it wander to a more serious, denser view if you wish to experience denser, heavier feelings. It's all simply a choice and "you" get to control where you go….

⁂

You have always known all that there possibly is to know. You carry within you vast amounts of information. Think of yourself as a vast field of intelligence and awareness. You have the ability to separate without really separating from the main field. It is more like a boundary that has been drawn around you to form an individual piece of God. It's very much like a hologram which contains all information of the whole in each tiny piece. You are pretty amazing in your ability to appear as separate just by expressing different parts of the whole.

You have this wonderful way of pretending to change from God light into human form. You are most imaginative and this imagination is a great asset in allowing you to change your thoughts. Imagine only the best, highest possible situations for any problem that you see. The greatest hurdle for you is that there are no problems – you are only focusing in a negative way. Always look for the long-term gift in any given situation.

Always know that everything is evolving and moving and changing as you evolve and move and change. When you stop moving and evolving and changing, you (your body) are in a comatose state and ready to leave earth. Stay changeable and flexible and you will be moving "with" the flow of life. Do not get stuck and stiff and rigid. You only become stiff and rigid in what you call death.

Now – you do not like to read about death and it is difficult for Liane to channel such information. Her body reacts to death with fear, as it has been programmed to do so. You all pretty much fear death and dying, and it is simply not necessary. You move on and you go within to where all information and intelligence is contained. There is no – I repeat – there is NO such thing as a devil or Satan, and there is no such place as hell. You are not judged at death, you are shown who you truly are and you are shown love. Some of you believe so strongly in hell fire and damnation that you may imagine such things to be true; however, they are not. You are shown as quickly as possible how things truly are, and you will find all information given to be most helpful in your transition. Do not fear death and you will find that you may actually make a transition that is quite peaceful with full awareness of where you are going. You don't really leave, as this is a made up dimension, or illusion, that you now live in; however, you feel like you are moving or transitioning into a brighter world.

I do not wish you to continue to fear death, as it does not serve you to do so. Allow death to be a passing from one room to another – now you see me, now you don't. You will find this crossing from one room to another to be most enlightening and often enjoyable. You may have read stories of near death experiences (NDE's) and these stories are true for each individual. Most see what they expect to see, until they are able to see more love and accept greater awareness. In this way each experience is a little different in the same way that all personalities are a little different.

The greatest part of the death experience is the great love and acceptance you may feel upon entry into this state of being. Remember – you are only going from one room, or dimension, to another – it is still you. You are an individual expression of God force even in death. You get to be you and you do not lose part of you, you only gain more awareness and you begin to see all differently. You will know how you do not sin and how there is no wrong way for energy to express.

Now; I do not want you to fear this information in any way whatsoever. You are aware enough now to not run in fear every time you feel your fear move in you. Acceptance and love are key here. Do not be afraid to lose your past programming that taught you to be afraid of being punished for being you. You will never ever be punished by God! This is the truth of the matter and it is time now that the truth prevails!

⁂

You have always been a loving light being and you have only forgotten that this is your true nature. It is what was intended when you entered this dimension. You must go unconscious in order to enter earth and the material world.

So, as you go unconscious, you literally shut down parts of yourself in order to slide easily "in" to this third dimension. Now is the time to "open" up to all that you truly are. Now is the time to know joy and bliss and all the gifts that come from being an unconditional loving being. So, do not be afraid to "accept" unconditionally until you can move up to loving unconditionally. I know you think it may be dangerous to be so open when you are constantly trying to protect yourself by shutting down, but opening up will allow you to accept God-you and to become all that you can be. You will love you by opening to love and you will free you by opening to love.

Be good to you and allow you to move at your own speed. Do not force yourself to open and do not push yourself. You will move with your desires – if the desire is in place wishing to rise higher, you will automatically begin to move in that direction. If the desire is to stay where you now are, you get to stay. It is all up to you and you may use your thoughts to move you in any direction you choose. You really do have a choice, actually you have many choices.

You are wonderful and magical and you have yet to discover how you create all that you see. Stay on the path and you will be guided to your requested destination. Know you are soul in a body and know that you came to earth by choice. You love it here and you love to return as often as possible. You are only beginning to discover all that you can be and you are only now beginning to bloom. You have spent your life growing and taking in information and rules and regulations, and now it is time to allow for no rules and no regulations. I do not mean for you to run out and break your laws; I mean that your beliefs are about to change as to how you may live within your laws with respect and acceptance, and yet not see your earth or country laws as your enemy. You put so much emphasis on danger and on fear of being controlled. You are a free spirit and you do not live out of fear... you flow "with" the energy and this is your power. You do not get upset when following man's rules; you simply accept that this will allow you to play in this dimension.

Please stop being so upset and angry about government and law enforcement, it is no different than being angry and upset with your neighbors. You are them and they are you. Also, when you are angry and upset it affects you... your body and your cells get to live in and exist in angry, dense energy. So, lighten up and live and let live. If you cannot coexist peacefully where you are, then I suggest you move. You may pack up and leave. This is a possibility and will assist you in finding an environment, or even a country, that is more conducive to you and your fears.

So; this leads us to immigration, which is difficult for you to deal with. Most of you know, before you even enter earth, which era you wish to live in. You are aware of the latest trends, wars and goings-on in this particular time. You are even aware of the rules and laws that prevail in your chosen era or time. You will find that you choose pretty much everything that goes with your chosen decade of entrance into earth. So you basically knew what would be going on after you arrived, just as you would if you had watched a movie first.

Now is the time to become the observer and look for the gift in all that you have chosen for yourself. Always flow with the energy of any situation until you see it move in a new direction. Always look for the gift and you will eventually find it. Always know that there is a gift, you are simply not aware of it at this time. Now – take everything I just wrote here and apply it to immigration, or any other "problem" you think you may be having at this time. There really are no problems, there is only energy changing and moving and shifting. Right now there is a giant shift occurring and you knew this before you came here to earth.

※

For the first time since you went unconscious, you will begin to see how you are much more than a human. You are actually part of God and you inhabit this body that you so casually walk around in. You are soul walking the earth and you are soul learning to operate in a very dense terrain. You are learning how to move forward from an unconscious state to a more aware, conscious state. You are like a child who is discovering its own fingers and toes. Next you will learn all the wonderful things you can do with these parts of yourself.

As you learn to walk (toes) and to use your hands (fingers), you will be most grateful to be alive and you will find it wonderful to discover your many talents and abilities. You are actually quite miraculous and you totally take it for granted that you can move around every day without thought. You take it for granted that you can see and hear and speak and think and smile and feel affection and love. You take it for granted and then you judge life if you begin to lose any of these abilities. You may even begin to judge God or yourself if you begin to lose your abilities that you so freely take for granted.

I would like you to begin to appreciate all that you now take for granted. I would like you to appreciate your fingers and toes and even your ideas and your thoughts. Just think – your thoughts can guide you in new directions and up to new dimensions of thought. Your thoughts are most important in steering you into acceptance and love or steering you into fear and paranoia. Your thoughts are most powerful and can change your mood from happy to sad or from sad to happy. Guide your thoughts toward happiness and joy as often as possible. This will allow these energies to grow bigger in your life. The more you send out (and in) the more you get back. Life truly is an echo, whatever you send out, you get back.

Now, as you grow deeper in love thoughts, you begin to stabilize in love. In the same way that you have grown into fear, you may grow into love. You simply fill your thoughts with love instead of filling your thoughts with fear. This allows you to stay in love without much effort; the echo that comes back to you will be more of the same. This is how magnetism works.

So now I have taught you the easiest way to get to love and to stay in love. This will allow you to have peace of mind no matter what is occurring in your outer world and this will allow you to stay calm no matter what is occurring in your outer world. The purpose of repeating this information to you, in so many different ways, is to reprogram your thinking in such a way as to allow you to live in a positive, happy life. You need not listen and you need not change just to make God, or a higher power, happy. God loves you just as you are right this minute. This information is not in the form of rules to live by, as there are no rules. You may freely choose how you wish to think and to play in this dimension, and you do not displease God ever! You may, however, displease yourself, and you are the one who is searching for help and for love and for guidance.

You will find your help and your love and even your guidance right inside of you, and your most helpful asset will be your thoughts. Do not worry; do not fear… you are on your way now. You are taking in positive information and this will guide you towards positivity. You will find that a diet of positive information is much more helpful to you than a diet of negative information. This is, of course, if your goal is to rise. If you wish to stay where you now are; continue doing and thinking as you always have.

You get to choose, you get to decide; you are driving you and moving you in any direction you choose. Be good to your body and love your thoughts and you will feel pretty good about being you… sweet, loving you….

*Y*ou are such a good version of yourself now, and you only judge you as not being your best. You find fault with yourself and you find fault with others. When you let go of this type of fault finding, you will let go of the weight of judgment that has held you down and away from the higher energies of joy and bliss. The only thing holding you down is judgment. Allow judgment to be a thing of the past by "choosing" acceptance.

Acceptance is your best friend. Acceptance leads to love, and unconditional love is the place you truly want to be. When you live in a state of unconditional love, you will feel so light and extremely happy. You will realize how everything is really in perfect divine order, and you will begin to draw to you all that is magnetized to the "vibration" of love. You will no longer draw the energies that are magnetized to judgment and criticism. You will have switched over to love, and love heals all. Do not fear if you do not drop all judgment immediately. Judgment has been your way of life since you entered this dimension, and it will take a little time to move judging aside and allow acceptance and love to take over.

Do not be afraid of love. Do not fear acceptance. Start small with little things and ideas until you can come to your center. Once you leave the fear side of you where you currently exist, you will find it easier and easier to accept life on life's terms. You are so afraid right now because your cells, which make up your body, are filled with much fear and are acting like a magnet to draw more fear to you. You can stop feeding yourself fear and this will help in your initial switch over to love. You may stop taking in information that stirs your fears. Fear is actually anything that is not love. Love is the other side of fear. Love is anything that uplifts and vibrates faster. Fear usually takes you down into the slower vibrating energies such as greater judgment and condemnation. Fear also contains revenge and anger and hatred... just to name a few. You will know, by how you feel, when you are in the higher vibrations of love, peace and calm. When you feel love, peace and calm, you will draw more of the same to you... it's that echo we talked about yesterday.

One way to know if you are feeding yourself higher vibrating information, in the way of thoughts and ideas, is to see if you feel really light in your decision. Sometimes, when you feel down it is because some part of you regrets your choice. It is okay to feel anything that you do feel, and it is helpful to learn to discern what you are currently feeling. Often, when you are healing and changing, you may feel energy that is leaving you, due to clearing and releasing old trapped energy from your cells. Do not worry when there is no immediate reason for dense emotions you may be feeling. Know that you are changing and growing in love. To grow in love is to move and shift energy. You are made of energy and you will feel these shifts within you. Often, when you don't feel well, you think you are getting sick. Sometimes, when you are releasing dense energy, you will feel it as it goes, and when it surfaces to be released it will affect you.

Not everything is energy coming into you. Sometimes it is energy leaving you. So, care for your emotions, and care for and nurture your body, and your psyche, as you release your fear and allow yourself to move to the higher vibrations while doing so.

You are loved and you are cared for more than you will know while in this dense dimension. You come from, and you belong to, a world of loving light, and you always return to this world of loving light. You are safe... you are loved and you are the best version of you at this time.

⚜

*Y*ou will find that you do not allow yourself many mistakes if you were severely punished as a child for your mistakes. Even if you saw others be severely punished for making mistakes, you may have developed a strong aversion to making your own mistakes. This leads to greater self-punishment for mistakes made. You may feel guilty after a conversation where you feel like you took over and were too aggressive. You may feel guilty after telling someone how stupid they are. You may even feel guilty after treating someone with impatience. All of these behaviors may cause you to punish yourself in some way, only because you "believe" that you have done wrong.

Your punishment may be as small as catching your finger in a drawer or as big as a headache. You may have allergies that act up when you believe you are stressed and overwhelmed. This may be a type of punishment for misbehavior, or it may be a result of not liking part of your self. You have many ways of punishing you and you have many thoughts and beliefs and also patterns that are buried in you.

You may release your need for punishment by releasing your guilt. Guilt draws punishment to you, so that you might feel like you have done penance for your sins. If you were raised in a religion that teaches you to repent for your sins, you may be more prone to a belief in self-punishment or an eye for an eye. This is what you are subconsciously doing. You are subconsciously punishing you for your sins or your mistakes.

We must get you to let go of all guilt in order to bring you out of self-harm and self-punishment. You are free to be you. You need not repent for making mistakes. You are not a sinner! You have never sinned and you are innocent! You need not apologize for your mistakes, and you are loved and cherished, and even revered, just the way you are. You are from God and part of God. How can you be so silly as to judge you? I will tell you how... you have been programmed and taught and trained to believe that you are a sinner and even that you are bad! You are not bad ever. You live in a world that tells you who you are, and this world is unconscious and unaware of the truth of the matter.

You are free to believe in your innocence. You are free to know the truth. You do not make mistakes and your life is not a mistake. Everything that you do, and everything that you are, is for a reason... you simply do not know what the reason is. You are doing what your soul came here to do. You are acting and behaving in a way that will work for you to get you where your soul intends you to be. I don't care if you went out and robbed a bank... you are following your path, your part, your role in this giant play or movie. Do not be upset with you and do not punish you. Love you and accept you just as you are, and you will be working with your soul and not struggling against the energy as you may now be doing.

You need not do anything except love you or like you just the way you are, and your energy will shift and you will begin to flow with life, instead of fighting and judging life. You can do this... you can easily come home to self-like and on to self-love. You are strong and you are healing with every bit of positive, uplifting information (which is energy taken in) that you read. Imagine – you may help heal you just by reading and feeding yourself positive instead of negative. There is no need to focus on what is considered wrong with the world when you have the choice to focus on what is right with the world and what is right with you.

Trust you and love you and know you. You are not who you were told. You are amazing and wonderful and very, very creative. Create your good now. Think positive thoughts about yourself and please let go of guilt!

~§~

*Y*ou have been on this journey of self-discovery for some time now and it is time to choose. You may choose to really know who you are and to accept your true reality, or you may stay in denial and continue on in unconsciousness. It's really a simple choice and you may simply say, "Yes, I wish to know who I am... please tell me." Or you may continue on as you have been and this too is acceptable.

You will find that the more curious you are, the more you learn or discover about the true nature of your personal reality. As you discover greater insights into the true nature of your personal reality, you will find yourself in confusion and seeking clarity for yourself. As you become clear on your chosen path, it is important to remember that "your path" is personal and may not suit another. You may be wound differently than your friends and your family. You may have been layered differently and you may require un-layering in your own personal way.

Think of energy as strings or even strong wire that has enveloped you over the years and even over lifetimes. This wire is all crisscrossed over you like a giant ball of string. In order to set you free of your restraints you must uncross all of these wires. One wire may need to go left and then right and then left again. It depends on how you took on this energy. So, if you tell your friends or family members that they need to do something specific, like move left or move right, it may not be the correct answer for them and they may become more tangled in energy.

All information given here is for you... not them. If you are reading these words right now it is because your guidance has brought you here. Do not force your way of unraveling your problems onto them. You are ready for this information or you would not have picked up this book to read my words. Allow your friends and your family to make their own choices and to be guided to the answers they are ready for. If you give this book, or any information, to a friend and they do not read it or follow it, that simply means it is not their way or is not their time. You do not force others to wake up to your truth or what works for you. In the same way, you may not force others to see life and situations as you see life and situations.

We have already determined that you see life through your own perspective, depending on how you are layered with your own fears. Have respect enough to allow others to have their own perspective, based on their own fears. Compassion is something that shows you how you understand how, or why, others might react or respond to situations the way that they choose to. You are walking your path and they are walking their own path. You all can't be teachers. We need cooks and police and firemen and lawyers and designers and artists and even law breakers to have a fully functioning play or movie. Let everyone play their part and you play yours.

You will find that others may ask for help from time to time in order to heal. They may be drawn to you for help or guidance, but this does not mean that you have the right to take over and begin to push them to be more like you. There is a fine line here between helping and controlling. Stay in your lane and do not feel superior or smarter than them. They are only acting and you are only acting. You are both God, so let it be. Let others be until you can wake up to who you truly are. You are not human and you never die. Do not pretend to be something you are not!

☙❧

*W*hen you begin to awaken, you will have strange feelings like you may be imbalanced. This is due to the fact that you are letting go of the old ways and thoughts and beliefs that have kept you off to one side of you... that fear side. So, as you come to center, you will feel that you are no longer fixed and you will be moving into a new, unused area of you.

As this occurs, you may become more sensitive than normal. This is not a problem, and you will feel more comfortable as you continue to think and feel from this newest shift to a higher level of vibration. Everything is always about vibration and drawing to you that which matches your current vibration. You will always magnetize to you that which you are putting out, and you will always feel that which you are releasing. For this reason you do not want to judge what you draw, or another way to put it is, you do not wish to draw what you are releasing; however, it is a good thing to release old trapped energy.

You are going to have your ups and downs for a while yet; however, as you release and clear more dense energy, you will become lighter and lighter in your vibration. You will begin to enjoy life more and more, and you will begin to shine your inner light a little more brightly. You will become aware of compassion and you will exude kindness more easily and readily. You will no longer require the approval of others and you will begin to approve of yourself. You will let go of self-judgment and self-criticism, and you will begin to feel better and less wounded. You will no longer require so much love and attention from others, as you will feel loved and approved of by your own self.

When you begin to feel trust and love for your own self, you will feel complete. You will feel accepted and you will feel comfortable with your own self. As you raise your vibration, you will become aware of your many assets and your many abilities. Things that you now take for granted will seem like huge gifts to you, and things that you now criticize will be seen as the gifts they truly are. You are on this path now. You are on your way to a whole new perspective. Do not give up. Continue to look for the good in absolutely everything and the good will be easier and easier to find. You do not need to continue to look for, and search out, the bad or the dangerous in order to protect yourself.

You are looking in a new direction now... you are looking for peace and harmony and you will wish to let go of your search for danger and even chaos. Look for the good and it will grow. Whatever you search for will get bigger and bigger. Whatever you put your energy into will grow exponentially. You are on your way now. Keep it positive and keep it good. You can do this. It's really not that difficult. Look for the good things in life, and in people, and you will find them. This is your new way of living on earth. This is how to use duality to rise above duality – you simply pick a side and use it to your advantage. Pick good – use good.

Now; when you decide to let go of fear, you will feel your fear leave you. It will rise to the surface after it has been released from your cells. Do not worry if you become very sensitive and fearful and nervous in your daily life. It is to be expected when fear is leaving. Know that you are always being guided and watched over, and know that you can simply ask your soul to guide you through your fearful moments. You are not alone in this. You are watched over by many, and you are part of the whole.

You will find that you will begin to move higher in vibration after each release of dense fear, and so you will feel lighter and lighter after a clearing of such energy. You are always guided, you are always loved and you are always part of God, the creator of all that is. You will do well with this rise up and you have already begun.

You have never been able to rise above the pull of the denser energies until now. Once you become aware of how you create, you will be able to stop yourself from going into these dense energies. As I have said repeatedly, it is a vibration and you will always draw to you that which matches your vibration. If you want to lift yourself up then raise your vibration and let your light shine.

You may move into love and joy and happiness simply by feeling love and joy and happiness. You may use affirmations to convince yourself that all is good and well and you are happy, or you may just focus on the idea of being joyful and happy and feeling good. Always assume that you will end up feeling better after any release of fear or anger or hurt. Always know that you are moving in a good direction with a good-for-you outcome at the end of any situation. Always put out that positive idea so that you receive positive back.

Now, if you feel down, do not fight it... allow the energy to release until you are drained of it, all the while knowing that this is a good thing and this will allow you to clear this vibrational down pull, so that you might be clear of it and rise higher after it is gone. You need not fight with energy that is leaving you, you may simply stay calm and breathe deep and maybe ask for guidance. If you have begun to communicate with your soul, it may be able to tell you how well you are doing with this process of clearing and releasing.

As you get lighter and lighter, it will be easier for you to keep your vibration up and to draw health and happiness to you. You will find that the more you clear those denser energies that weigh you down, the easier it becomes to love you and to like you and to accept you. And once you are sending out the message "I love me," you will receive love back. When you send love out into the world, even self-love, you receive love back. Creating is really so simple once you get the hang of it and let go of your blocks to your own good.

So today, I would like you to know that you are loved and you are liked and you are happy and you are full of joy. Now – repeat that to yourself all day today. "I am loved, I am liked, I am happy and I am full of joy!" If you wish to add some power to this affirmation you may wish to write it one hundred times. You see, writing something down involves your hand and your arm and your mind and your heart that pumps the blood to all of these. It is very powerful and will give you results faster.

So, have a very good vibration day by speeding up your process and by vibrating in positivity.

※

For the most part you have done well on your journey into the material world. Now it is time to remember your true nature which is an expression of God. Please begin to see how you can rise above this material world to new heights. Please begin to know how you are spirit in human form. Please begin to realize how everyone is spirit in human form.

You are all just working on awakening, so that you might show yourselves how love works and how love is the only way if you wish to go higher and higher. Love will lift you up and love will solve any problem you may have. You have gotten lost in this game that you play and love is your way back home. You think everything is bad and in chaos, simply because you are changing and growing and moving in a new direction. You see hate and anger as terrible and so you see people and life as terrible. What if hate is only fear built up and projected out? What if anger is only a response to fear, and what if you can see it all differently? What if the answer is to watch these energies until they change? What if the answer to chaos is to stay calm and wait for this energy to pass? What if when you join in the chaos, by adding greater or more anger, you cause it to expand and to grow? You may keep anger and fear growing by making it bigger. You make it bigger by adding more to it!

Remove yourself from the fight! See all as working out well and become the observer. Do not make decisions based on fear, and know that all is well and is really moving in a good direction. You do not see the whole picture, and you do not understand the wonderful times that you are in because you are looking for the wrong thing. When you spend your life looking for ways to protect yourself from danger you must first identify what danger is. This causes you to search out dangerous ideas and dangerous thoughts and dangerous rules and dangerous people. You basically become a heat seeking missile looking for and intently focused on "danger." It's time now to let it all go and to realize how everything is only here to entertain you, and how you set up this game so you could enjoy being in a body and living in this material world, or this dream world.

It is safe now to know the truth. You are safe! You do not die... you do not end. You come here again and again, often with the goal of creating heaven on earth. Play that role. You are the sole/soul creator of your reality, and you have the ability to make it anything you want it to be. Just ask to be shown love... ask to be shown heaven. Ask to let go of your search for danger and begin to see how safe you really are. You are blowing danger way out of proportion, and it is time now to calm down and realize how you are a creator and to "wake up" to the fact that you create every minute of every day. You create! Begin to create what you want. If you want to live in a world of fear and danger, you know how to do that really well. If, however, you wish to create a world of peace and love for yourself, you might want to shift your perspective from fear and danger to love and peace.

It's all your choice. You get to decide if you are ready to see life in a whole new way, or if you wish to continue on with fear. You are God and you create. You came from God and you are part of God. You are a drop from the ocean of All That Is and you contain all parts of the ocean. You are never-ending loving light energy and you are pretending that you are something else. Be you... be the real you! Know yourself. Wake up and begin to love!

⚛

*Y*ou have always wanted to explore and to find new ways of living and of creating in your lives. This is a time of great exploration into your own self. You always want to know how things work and you care little about how you work. You are basically unknown to you. You understand how your organs and other vital parts function, however, you do not know much beyond that. Your doctor takes care of the big issues and you take care of the little ones.

You have much to learn about living in a body with a mind and a personality and set of beliefs. It is time now to entertain the fact that you are much greater than you realize. It is time now to grow beyond ignorance and to accept that you are more complex than anyone has told you. You have the ability to create in many different ways and you are totally unaware that you do. Because of your unconscious state, you will move slowly into awareness. Slow, steady movement is necessary to allow you to wake up without jarring your senses. You are semi-conscious and you do not wish to frighten yourself deeper into unconsciousness. This is why it is important not to push your self or to push others. Everything is working in a gradual, smooth operation that will assist you as you come awake.

You are not to push information at others in an effort, or your need, to wake them early. They are working on their schedule, not yours. So, allow everyone to be and you continue on with your own awakening. You will find that the others will be most grateful that you allowed them to sleep in for a while. You are not to be frustrated with them for what you call "their ignorance." This is causing problems for you and you do not wish to carry all that judgment in you.

So; we have discussed your need to have everyone see life your way, and now we will discuss being on the receiving end of such behavior, when it has not been requested. You will find that when others push you to change or to see life as they see life, you may feel defensive. This defensiveness may lead to hurt feelings. It may feel like they are telling you how stupid you are or it may feel like they don't like you. What they don't like is how you believe and how you see life. Do not worry that they will harm you for your beliefs, as that is what you mostly fear. Stay in your heart and allow for change and allow for diversity. Allow yourself to move away from anyone who feels that you are not good enough the way that you are. Remember too that others may move away from you, if they do not feel that you accept them the way that they are.

You do not control others and you are not in charge of others. You are "in" you and you get to drive you around all day. Do not be so arrogant as to believe you may incringe on the behavior of another. Now; when you do things to help others who are requesting help, it is okay to give the help they request without forcing them to change their beliefs. You are all confused when it comes to religion and religion does not always serve you. Think twice before joining any group who tells you how to think and how to believe. Use only the highest form of philosophy and choose thoughts that do not put others down. If you wish to rise above duality, it is best to rise above any sort of judgment and condemnation. You are innocent and all others are innocent. I know this is difficult to believe, however, it is the truth.

So; make sure you allow for all to be God... not just you. And make sure to allow for all to be innocent... not just you. You will get the hang of coming out of duality; it is just a matter of time and a matter of rising up to a higher perspective. You will get there if your desire is to go higher. You will always arrive right where you wish to go. You are moving up, and to do so requires letting go of some old, traditional beliefs. It's a choice you make and it is your choice... no pressure will ever be put on you because you are God, expressing through matter in any way that you wish. Be you, follow you and love and accept all that you are. You are moving in a new direction that allows for love and acceptance of all that is. You will lift higher as you release your weight of judgment. You will rise up to the next dimension when you release your hold on this dimension.

Rise higher and enjoy the gifts at the higher levels or stay here for a while and sleep. It is good to sleep too… it's all good!

᠁

*Y*ou have always known that you are a spirit, you only forgot. You somehow decided it was more fun to come to earth with no prior knowledge of your existence in the spirit realms. You wanted to have no memory of all that you do as a spirit, and you wanted to be unaware of your connection to and from God.

So now you sit here and you feel lost and alone. You are not really lost and you are never alone. You are part of All That Is and you contain all the information that exists within the field of All That Is. You are part of everything and you are watched over and you are guided and you are loved. You only need to reconnect with you… the soul in you. You only need to return to that part of you that is love and trust and joy. You only need to let go of your desire for pain and struggle that has been brought on by your need for punishment – which has been brought on by your desire to judge and criticize. You will find that judgment is deeply rooted in you and it will take some time to let it go and to release it. Be very patient with yourself as you allow judgment to leave. Allow all to occur and you will assist judgment on its way out of you.

Once you have released judgment, you will be well on your way to returning to your natural state of being. You will arrive in a state of love and pleasure that is unknown to you now. You will feel so free and so happy when your vibration rises and you will know love and joy. You will live a life of happiness with a peace that is unknown to most of you now. You will be a very happy soul, and you will feel gratitude for things and situations that you once judged. Everything will change simply because your perspective will have changed. You will wake up happy and excited to see what the new day has brought you. You will no longer fight with yourself and you will no longer fight with others. You will let go of your need to be right and to prove others wrong. This need is based on low self-esteem and on a fear of being punished for being wrong.

You will no longer fear being wrong, and you will just "know" that everything is okay and you are okay and life is okay and evolution is okay. You actually fear evolution because you fear change. You do not like change, as you do not understand change. You only see what you are losing and now you will begin to see what you are gaining. You have a great deal to learn about love and acceptance, and I hope you continue on this path towards these two gifts. You may add so much to your life by simply opening up and accepting. Right now you are very closed down; and when you reject life you are basically rejecting you. You are life. You are part of All That Is and you are part of all that is here. Do not kill off parts of you out of fear. Allow you to be all that you are and allow you to live to your fullest potential.

Everything is okay and you are okay. Everything is acceptable and you are acceptable. I will continue to tell you how wonderful you are until you get it. Know that you are God... know that you are love... and know that you are evolving into your true self by letting go of everything that is holding you back. You are so much more than you now realize, and you are moving into a new form of you that will allow you to see how great of a soul you truly are. You are so close now. Continue to learn about life and love, and continue to evolve in an upward direction. I have given you the thought and the ideas that will assist you in turning direction and moving into your new upward journey. Do not let go now. Continue upward and ask your soul to guide you. You and your soul are connected... you are one. You came here to earth, and now you will become "aware" that there is more to you than this human who is being guided to read these words.

Keep going... do not give up! You are God... you are soul... you are very, very special and you are waking up to the fact that you are. I love you and I will assist you when you need me to. Just ask. I am you... you are me... we are one.

·❧·

$\mathscr{A}$s you continue to rise up, you will begin to see how you are a soul and a spirit being. You will let go of your need to judge anything, as you will have reconnected with the part of you who is unconditional love and light. You will know intuitively that all is well and that you are always loved and always cared for. You will open to the part of "you" that loves and cares for yourself.

As this evolution occurs, you will begin to relax into life, and so your personal reality will become relaxed and less tense. There will be less pressure on you to perform and to act a certain way. There will be less stress in your life due to the added acceptance and love. You all want to be accepted and love is your true nature. When you feel accepted you put your defenses down. When you feel accepted, you feel loved and you give love more freely. Love and acceptance are two great healers and will allow you to totally enjoy your life. You will feel changed and you will feel so much lighter with less confusion. You will be in heaven and you will enjoy life as never before. It only takes letting go of your weight belt and allowing all judgment to leave you.

Now – as you let go of judgment you may feel it as it leaves your cells, so do not worry when you feel like you may be slipping back into judgment. This is a time to stay calm and sit down and breathe. You will find that you will learn how to clear and release your no longer needed energies in a positive fashion, simply by giving them time to leave you. We are not running a race here and this is not a competition. This is a process of ascension, and all is going well so far with this move to an upward direction.

So; do not judge you and do not judge the others among you, who may be moving and changing and in confusion. All is well and all has been well for some time now. You just have blinders on and so you cannot see how well and good this evolution process is. Your job is to allow and accept, and then, when you get there, to embrace life on earth. You are creating a wonderful event and all is well on earth at this time!

I will now end this book with my all-time favorite saying... God bless you!

"We don't see things as they are; we see them as we are."
–Anais Nin

Epilogue

You have not understood much of what I have written here, as it is difficult for you to see yourself as God. I will continue to write through Liane and hopefully she will share this gift with you.

You have been on this path to discovery for some time now and you will always be guided to your highest good. You need not worry if you do not feel your God connection, or even your soul connection, right away. These things take time, and you have been searching for your answers and receiving what you will allow to come to you. Do not be afraid that you will never achieve your success. You are being assisted in many ways and on many levels. There are so many in the spirit realms that love and support you and even are part of you. You are never ever alone, and you are always loved and watched over and even guided by those who watch over you.

It is simply a matter of getting through to you and of being received. Try to stay open when it comes to unknown information and the paranormal. So many are taught to fear the unknown, and this may put up blocks for you to receive certain, specific information... it is just too far-out sounding to you, and you do not want to become weird or strange or an outcast. Even Liane writes under a pseudonym to retain her privacy and prevent those, who may not agree with her work, from criticizing. It is not easy to break away from what is considered normal behavior and move into the unknown.

So I would like to say "thank you," to those of you who are brave enough to break away from the normal pack thinking and venture into the unknown. In time this information will become common knowledge, but for now it is new and enlightening and, in some cases, even eye opening. You will find that as you continue to receive opening information, you will continue to open you up to receive even more. You get what you look for and what you search for... remember that! If you search for the good you will find it and if you search for the bad, you will find it. Stay where you feel best. Your sense of well-being is most important for your healing.

This is good for now. I hope to write for you again soon....

God

"We are slowed down sound and light waves, a walking bundle of frequencies tuned into the music of the cosmos, we are souls dressed up in sacred biochemical garments, and our bodies are the instruments through which our souls play their music."

– Unknown

God's Pen

I first heard the voice of God in 1988. I was sitting in my back yard reading a book when this big booming voice interrupted with, "I am God and I will not come to you by any other name." I felt like the voice was everywhere – inside of me as well as in the sky around me. I was so frightened that I ran in my bedroom to hide.

This was not the first time that I heard voices. I had been communicating with my own spirit guide or soul for about a year. I guess my depth of fear regarding God, and all that he represented to me at the time, was just too much.

I spent two days trying to avoid the voice of God, which was patiently waiting for me to respond. By the second day I was exhausted from lack of sleep and decided to give in and talk with him. This turned out to be the greatest gift and best decision of my life.

In the beginning the voice of God would wake me in the middle of the night and tell me it was time to write. He said I had promised to do this work (I assumed he was talking about the soul/spirit me). I would drag myself up to a sitting position and watch in amazement as my hand flew across the page, while I tried to keep up by reading what was being written.

It was always so much fun to wake up the next morning and grab my notebook to see what God had written during the night. After some time the voice stopped waking me and I became comfortable picking up my pen and writing for God first thing in the morning. I think in the beginning I had to be awakened while still semi-conscious from sleep so I wouldn't object too much to the information that was being channeled through me.

As I grew less and less afraid (and more trusting) of God, he was able to communicate greater information. Some of the information is quite controversial, but I felt it important to just let it be and not censor it. I present the writings in this book to you as they were given to me.

For privacy reasons I am using a pen name. I asked God for a good pen name and he guided me to Liane which (I was told) in Hebrew means "God has answered."

At one point I became a little concerned about my sanity in all this, so I went to a hypnotherapist to find out what I was doing. Under hypnosis I saw this incredibly huge beam of light with a voice coming from within it. It was a giant "loving light" and felt so comforting and kind. It felt like that's where I came from. After that I stopped worrying about my sanity. If this is crazy, I think it's a very good kind of crazy to be....

In loving light, *Liane*

Ram Dass Quotes

"We're all just walking each other home."

"Treat everyone you meet like God in drag."

Introduction to
The Loving Light Books Series

There are many ways to go within to your core or your heart center. When you reach deep within your own psyche you will enter the core of your being. This is where soul and spirit resides.

For those of you who wish to reconnect with your own God self I highly suggest that you read and reread the Loving Light Books Series. This series is designed to draw you "within" to your own God self and to allow you to peel away the layers that prevent you from becoming the loving, radiant being that you truly are.

This series of 20 books was received by my pen (Liane) over a 10 year span of time and are quite remarkable. You will be led from an earthly way of viewing life to a more God-like way of viewing life. Everything is subjective in this three-dimensional world that you now call home. You, however, are a spiritual being and your life as a human is out of balance since you decided to enter matter. We will feed you information in this series that will allow you to *perceive* your current life in a whole new way.

These books were written for my channel and are most helpful to anyone who wishes to add more love and understanding to their life here on earth. If you are happy with where your life stands now, I do wish you well. If, on the other hand, you would like to learn more about your own spirit essence and how to connect with the part of you that draws love and unconditional light into your life, I highly suggest you begin your journey *within* by reading these helpful books.

I wish you well on your journey to discovering "you"....

God

Loving Light Books

Book 1: God Spoke through Me to Tell You to Speak to Him
Book 2&3: No One Will Listen to God & You are God
Book 4: The Sun and Beyond
Book 5: The Neverending Love of God
Book 6: The Survival of Love
Book 7: We All Go Together
Book 8: God's Imagination
Book 9: Forever God
Book 10: See the Light
Book 11: Your Life as God
Book 12: God Lives
Book 13: The Realization of Creation
Book 14: Illumination
Book 15: I Touched God
Book 16: I and God are One
Book 17: We All Walk Together
Book 18: Love Conquers All
Book 19: Come to the Light of Love
Book 20: The Grace is Ours

Also by Liane Rich

The Book of Love (Includes: For the Love of God)
For the Love of God: An Introduction to God
For the Love of Money: Creating Your Personal Reality
Your Individual Divinity: Existing in Parallel Realities
For the Love of Life on Earth
Your Return to the Light of Love: a guidebook to spiritual awakening
Journey into Your Soul: finding your true self

Loving Light Books

Available at:
Loving Light Books: www.lovinglightbooks.com
Amazon: www.amazon.com
Also on request at local bookstores